MARCO  POLO

C000304104

LAS VEGAS

CANADA

Washington

Montana

North Dakota

Oregon

Idaho

South Dakota

California

Wyoming

Nebraska

Iow

Nevada

Denver

USA

Las Vegas

Utah

Colorado

Kansas

M

Los Angeles

Arizona

Oklahoma

A

PACIFIC OCEAN

New Mexico

Texas

MEXICO

www.marco-polo.com

The best Insider Tips → p. 4

INSIDER TIP

Best of ... → p. 6

Sightseeing → p. 26

Food & Drink → p. 50

SYMBOLS

INSIDER TIP	Insider Tip
★	Highlight
● ● ● ●	Best of ...
⛰	Scenic view
🕓	Responsible travel: fair trade principles and the environment respected

PRICE CATEGORIES HOTELS

Expensive over 165 dollars

Moderate 100–165 dollars

Budget under 100 dollars

Prices are valid for a double room without breakfast (prices differ according to season and day)

PRICE CATEGORIES RESTAURANTS

Expensive over 35 dollars

Moderate 20–35 dollars

Budget under 20 dollars

Prices are valid for a main meal at night, including tax and 15% tip, lunches are cheaper

On the cover: Gamble like a professional – rules and tips p.88 | Las Vegas Special – I do! p.93

CONTENTS

Shopping → p. 62

Entertainment → p. 68

Where to stay → p. 78

Street atlas → p. 108

DID YOU KNOW?

MAPS IN THE GUIDEBOOK

(110 A1) Page numbers
and coordinates refer to
the street atlas
(O) Site/address located off
the map. Coordinates are also
given for places that are not
marked on the street atlas

A public transportation route
map can be found inside the
back cover. A map of Las
Vegas and surround can be
found on p. 116/117

**INSIDE BACK COVER:
PULL-OUT MAP →**

PULL-OUT MAP ⌖

(⌖ A–B 2–3) Refers to the
removable pull-out map

2 | 3

The best MARCO POLO Insider Tips

Our top 15 Insider Tips

INSIDER TIP Reggae in the desert

Hot beats, Caribbean food and drinks: every year in June, the Reggae Festival attracts punters with popular Jamaican musicians like Freddie McGregor → p. 99

INSIDER TIP Fancy dress

The fun starts in the fitting room: feather boas, hats and glitzy clothes from stage shows. You will find the best selection of crazy second-hand things at The Attic → p. 65

INSIDER TIP Stay cool

The latest trend: parties and discos at the swimming pool. Exactly what you need in the hot Las Vegas summer → p. 75

INSIDER TIP The desert blooms

Flash floods and straw walls: the Springs Preserve has interactive displays that show natural history and environmental issues in interesting and exciting ways for children → p. 45

INSIDER TIP Good ol' times

Golden Gate is Downtown's oldest and smallest hotel. Its elegant furnishings, dimly lit corridors and antique Victorian ornaments all combine to evoke the casinos of yesteryear → p. 86

INSIDER TIP Something serious

Documents, photos and statements from former employees are on display in the Atomic Testing Museum. They demonstrate the astonishing naivety of early atomic research when postcards with photos of the explosion were popular → p. 44

INSIDER TIP Dive the Titanic

The luxury liner has been lying on the bottom of the Atlantic for 100 years. The Titanic exhibition in the Luxor tells its story with displays including a gigantic part of the ship's side, replicas of some of the rooms (photo left) as well as personal items belonging to passengers, like glasses and clothing → p. 30

BEST OF ...

FOR FREE

● *The Strip by night*
Strolling along the brightly-lit Las Vegas Boulevard at night is a unique experience that takes you past the Statue of Liberty, the Eiffel Tower, gigantic billboards and lakes. In the centre is *Sirens of TI*, a show on the Strip where you can watch a ship sinking → p. 38

● *Rock around the clock*
In the lounges of the large casinos some very good up-and-coming bands often perform for free. So try places like the *Scene Lounge* in the Venetian or the *Koi Lounge* at Planet Hollywood for some live music → p. 75

● *Photo safari in the casino*
Whilst the tiger in the Mirage can only be viewed from behind bars, the *MGM Casino* shows their wild cats completely free. There is a glass enclosure in the centre of the casino with a pride of lions and they can even be viewed from underneath in a glass tunnel (photo below) → p. 31

● *Play of water*
Every evening the water fountains in front of the *Bellagio* dance to the music of Pavarotti, Céline Dion and the Vienna Philharmonic. Every 15 minutes the 1200 jets perform an impressive, choreographed water ballet of light and music on a massive artificial lake on the Strip → p. 34

● *Vintage nostalgia*
1950 Chevys, Cadillacs and antique Fords and even one of Elvis' original cars, are all on show at the Imperial Palace – a car buff's dream. Download a coupon from the *Auto Collections* website and book a free entrance ticket → p. 34

● *Hoover's walls*
The *Hoover Dam* is one of the wonders of the modern world. With all the concrete used to build the dam, you could build a road from New York to San Francisco. You have to pay for a tour but the breathtaking view from the bridge makes it worthwhile → p. 48

● ● ● ● Dots in guidebook refer to 'Best of ...' tips

● *The players from above*

The tower of the *Stratosphere Casino* (photo right) offers the most panoramic view of the city and the desert. At 1148ft it also offers action-packed attractions and thrilling rides → p. 40

● *Get married in the city of lights*

In a helicopter, barefoot next to the swimming pool or in a wonderfully kitschy chapel – tie the knot! Getting married in Las Vegas has its own style and it is fast and cheap. Almost 100,000 couples a year cannot be wrong . . . → p. 93

● *Light show over the pedestrian zone*

Stars, crosses and triangles fly through the heavens, while a rock band sets the rhythm for the lights: the *Fremont Street Experience* light show makes a trip Downtown worthwhile → p. 42

● *Tiger in the Mirage*

Even though Siegfried & Roy no longer perform, their rare white tigers can still be admired – they are an attraction in the *Mirage Casino* where these remarkable wild animals live in a very luxurious enclosure → p. 37

● *Elvis lives!*

The latest trend is music shows – Sinatra, the Beatles etc. But Elvis, with his legendary rhinestone costumes, was a very special star for the city and that is what makes the revival show 'Viva Elvis' in the Aria worth seeing → p. 77

● *Be a high roller*

Blackjack, roulette, poker – these are the games of luck which brought Las Vegas into existence. So get playing! Of course, you will have to sacrifice a few dollars to lady luck but she may well smile upon you and you could win the jackpot → p. 88

● *Satisfy your hunger*

Not all of the legendary Las Vegas buffets are worth the money. One that certainly is, is the *Bellagio*: fresh pasta, sushi, mussels, bison meat and over 100 other dishes are displayed in an array of hot and cold spreads → p. 53

ONLY IN

BEST OF ...

● *Which way to the swimming pool?*
It is unimaginable for any hotel in Las Vegas not to have a swimming pool but for some extra fun you should visit *Mandalay Bay*. An aquatic playground in 11 acres with a wave swimming pool, a sandy beach, a variety of swimming pools and even a 'river' → p. 84

● *Cool shopping*
Sample some perfumes, browse for some shoes or shop for some designer outfits: the *Fashion Show Mall* entices with almost 2 million square feet of air-conditioned shopping fun (photo left) → p. 65

● *Sparkling show*
When the performers of the Cirque du Soleil's water show 'O' dive into the huge lake with a flourish, you too will feel the soothing coolness of the water. Watching the show is refreshing and the air-conditioning does the rest → p. 77

● *Cool in the Colorado*
Beneath the Hoover Dam the Colorado River stays quite cool even during midsummer, because the river comes from the depths of Lake Mead. Hire a boat or a canoe at *Willow Beach* for a refreshing excursion → p. 49

● *Icy art indulgence*
A cool experience is guaranteed in the city wonderland of the *Minus 5 Ice Bar* at Mandalay Bay, you will be surrounded with ice sculptures whilst you sip your cocktails at minus 5 degrees – from a glass made of ice → p. 71

● *Oasis in the desert*
When the mercury rises over 40° C/104° F degrees and you are close to collapsing, enjoy a stay at a lake close to the city. The luxurious *Loews Lake Las Vegas Resort*, built in a Moroccan style, has large swimming pools, slow swaying palms and golf greens → p. 80

HEAT

●●●● Dots in guidebook refer to 'Best of ...' tips

RELAX AND CHILL OUT
Take it easy and spoil yourself

● *Mud and honey*

The spa treatments at the *Sahra Spa & Hammam* at the Cosmpolitan Hotel ranges from vigorous hammam massages to soothing mud and honey packs. The swimming pool area also offers you one of the best views of the Strip → **p. 37**

● *A margarita at sunset*

A seaplane hangs from the ceiling, old fishing boats are used in the seating area and the margaritas get mixed in a 'volcano'. *Margaritaville* evokes the chilled-out Florida Keys and is a very relaxing place for a sundowner. Catch the sunset from the terrace → **p. 71**

● *Ultimate luxury in swimming pools*

Hotel swimming pools are important in Las Vegas – so you can relax and recover after the long nights. Ancient Rome inspired the five elegantly designed swimming pools at the *Bellagio.* Or you can spoil yourself in their award-winning spa → **p. 44**

● *Picnic in the desert*

The humming air-conditioners, the constant clatter of the one-arm bandits – sometimes you just long for some silence in Las Vegas. Take a break from it all and have a picnic out amongst the red sandstone cliffs of the *Valley of Fire* → **p. 49**

● *Off to the salt cave*

The *Canyon Ranch Spa Club* occupies an entire floor at the Venetian so it is no wonder that, besides saunas and Ayrveda massage rooms, they also have enough space for a salt cave and two restaurants – lots room to relax → **p. 44**

● *Over the roofs of Las Vegas*

An elegant cocktail, a fabulous view of the lights of the Strip: here you can start – or end – a sophisticated evening in a relaxed atmosphere. The *Mix-Lounge* (photo left) is located high in THEhotel tower of the Mandalay Bay and it even has a balcony → **p. 72**

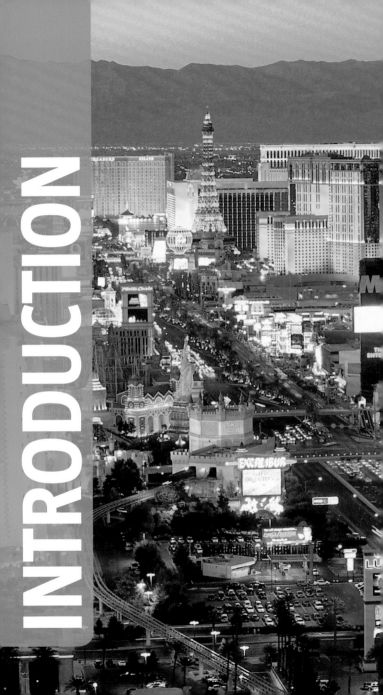

INTRODUCTION

DISCOVER LAS VEGAS!

Las Vegas is not actually a real city but rather the embodiment of the American dream of instant gratification, a neon Fata Morgana in the desert. Las Vegas lives on the dreams and obsessions of people in search of instant wealth and instant gratification. This driving desire is why a city could rise out of the sand – in the middle of the barren, scorching heat of the southern Nevada desert – and become the world's gambling centre. Around the clock, 365 days a year, this gambling city is a glittering fantasy world that makes the reality of everyday life, seem very far away.

Time and space become meaningless in the neon oasis of Las Vegas. The Downtown casinos, and those on Las Vegas Boulevard and the legendary Strip, transport you to another reality, to an artificial air-conditioned world. Here you will find yourself in ancient Rome, or strolling through New York, Venice or through a fairy tale medieval castle. Even during the recession, new and more spectacular casino palaces are being built and more exciting shows and illusions are offered.

Photo: View over the Strip

Annually, almost 40 million visitors flood the glittering metropolis in the Mojave Desert but the property and financial crisis of the past few years has curtailed the length of visitors' stay and they are not as generous as they were at the gambling tables. Today, most visitors stay three or four nights – and you will need at least that length of time if you want to see all the various aspects of the city. A lot of visitors, especially Americans, often come back, allowing themselves a short break from their everyday routines to try their luck: gambling, winning, losing, watching the shows, spending the nights in hot clubs and cool bars. Or they relax at the swimming pools and spas, go dining or simply let the flashing neon lights and LED screens on the Strip and Downtown carry them away.

Cheap rip-offs and sophisticated entertainment

Las Vegas offers both cheaply produced rip-offs as well as sophisticated entertainment. Shows are produced using the latest technology and shows like the Cirque du Soleil are experiences that involve all the senses. Wild roller coaster rides, white tigers and lions all ensure non-stop action and a feeling of the exotic. There are museums and galleries that exhibit works of world-renowned artists and even some of the casinos themselves are works of art. And there are many sophisticated restaurants that inspire the eyes as well as the palate.

For a long time Las Vegas was the fastest growing city in the USA and today it has almost 2 million citizens. Lured by work opportunities in the casino industry, almost 80,000 people a year moved to Clark County (Las Vegas and its immediate surroundings) between 1990 and 2008. This is where the American dream – where taxi drivers can make millions, and hotel porters line their pocket and own villas – can become a reality. However, the recent recession has put a huge damper on the boom town. House and property prices have dropped by 50 per cent and the unemployment rate has soared to a staggering 15 per cent. Thousands have moved away – and even left their houses and mortgages behind.

The irony of fate: the men who founded this glittering world were actually Mormons. Around 1830, Mexican traders discovered a small oasis with an artesian well at the foot of the Spring Mountain. The name Las Vegas, which translates as the 'plains', dates back to that time. In 1855, the Mormons built a small fort to protect their wagon trails on their way to the Pacific. But it was only in 1905, that Las Vegas came into being, it developed from a workers' camp for the first railroad in the region. Saloons and gambling halls (at that time they were still illegal) sprouted up along the dusty Fremont Street in front of the train station to form the basis of a fledgling city.

1931 became the year of fortune for Las Vegas. The state of Nevada legalised gambling (officially to cash in on tax money for schools). At the same time, the US government started building the Hoover Dam on the Colorado River. Soon, 5000 workers were living in camps on the outskirts of the city – and Las Vegas boomed in the middle of a worldwide economic crisis. New casinos sprang up in the desert sands and by 1940 the population had risen to 8500 inhabitants. The Second World War brought soldiers

The legendary 'Welcome to Fabulous Las Vegas' neon sign

and the arms industry, but also danger: for ten years underground atomic tests were conducted only 70 miles from the city. The tests themselves even became an attraction for the casino guests.

Of course, the American Mafia (the Mob) could not just sit by and ignore such a lucrative little city. A gang war erupted between the followers of Al Capone and Lucky Luciano – the Mafia clans from Chicago and New York – over casino profits. In 1946, the notorious Benjamin (Bugsy) Siegel opened the Flamingo with star guest Frank Sinatra. The Flamingo was the first luxury casino on the Strip, the main thoroughfare leading to Los Angeles. The Flamingo failed and went bankrupt and Bugsy was eventually killed by a hit man.

> A Mafia war erupted around the casino profits

The era of glamorous entertainment started in the 1950s and this was the time for which Las Vegas became famous, the era of Elvis Presley and the Rat Pack with Sinatra, Dean Martin and Sammy Davis Jr. A gambling commission controlled gambling and issued licences and the government declared war on organised crime. For decades the FBI investigated these powerful illegal syndicates. During the 1970s various instigators were arrested for cashing in on the profits of casino revenues. Some politicians were suspected of being in cahoots with the Mob and in the 1980s a series of murders in the area were clearly the Mafia's responsibility.

Downtown in Fremont Street, you can still imagine how Las Vegas must have been in its heyday, when the main pleasure was gambling, drinking and smoking – and a visit to a 'working girl' afterwards.

Since then, Las Vegas has expanded its entertainment range. Everybody still comes to gamble, but in Vegas there is also far more drinking, partying and prostitution (even though it is illegal), than in any other American city. But even holidaymakers, who frown upon these indulgences, get their money's worth here.

New casinos: each more splendid and fanciful than the last

Each new casino built was more splendid, more fanciful that the last. In 1973, the MGM was the largest hotel in the world with 2100 rooms. In 1990, Excalibur took the honours with 4032 rooms until the MGM Grand reclaimed the title again with 5000 rooms. Almost every year, one of the casinos expands with a new tower and space for a thousand more guests. Today, there are almost 150,000 rooms in the city. Most of the hotel giants belong to large consortiums, which call many of these large casinos their own.

Elvis became the King in Las Vegas and you can still admire his 1951 Cadillac

A lot of building projects were halted during the recession. But it is not only the ongoing financial crisis that has endangered the development of the city. Las Vegas and the entire south-western USA, is threatened by a drought. The reservoir of the Hoover Dam with the largest man-made lake in America, Lake Mead, is running dry. The lake has dropped to almost half of its capacity. The water level has not been this low in the last thirty years. With the snow melt in 2011, the Colorado River brought some water down from the Rockies, but the drought conditions of the past ten years continue.

At the same time the river has to provide more and more people with water and energy. Only a small percentage of the water is pumped to Las Vegas, the lion's share of the Colorado water is used for agricultural purposes, irrigating the barren lands of Arizona, South California and Nevada. The alarm bells are finally sounding: if the drought persists, the Hoover Dam turbines will have to be shut off, and along with it, the power supply. A catastrophe that will also affect all the neighbouring states.

> **Las Vegas is under a 'drought watch'**

In Las Vegas, people have started to take action and a 'drought watch' has been declared with strict water regulations being enforced for the watering of lawns, washing of cars and use of decorative fountains. There are restrictions on new buildings being constructed and the building of new swimming pools is completely forbidden. However, tourism is mostly spared from these restrictions. Businesses on the Strip and Downtown all have special exemptions and so people continue to live the high life, the precious water is lavishly squandered and the energy-sapping neon lights shimmer day and night.

Nobody wants to believe the depressing predictions and nobody comes to Vegas to listen to gloomy apocalyptic theories. Even those people, who arrive in Sin City with a sceptical frown, succumb in the end to the seductions of this fantastic wonderland. Because Las Vegas is unique. It is like a kitsch and surreal film – where the visitors are allowed to partake in the act – but for this you will have to sacrifice quite a few dollars to fortune.

WHAT'S HOT

1 Get stuck right in

Fast food You do not have your food on plastic trays in Vegas' modern fast food palaces. At *Le Burger Brasserie* you will have the best meat and the freshest salad ever served between two slices of bread. Or why not try some Kobe beef and Maine lobster *(the Paris Las Vegas, 3655 Las Vegas Blvd)*? Even at *Sammy's,* fast food and luxury go together quite happily: try the pizza with truffle oil and imported brie *(6500 W. Sahara Ave)* while over at *Stack* in the *Mirage,* lobster tacos with mango and coriander is the dish to go for *(3400 S. Las Vegas Blvd)*.

In the basket

2

Sporty Not only do you need a basket for basketball, but you also have to get the disc to land in the basket with disc golf, a game that is played at the *Mountain Crest Park (Durango Rd)* and *Sunset Park (Sunset Rd)* and sometimes also at night under artificial lighting. If you prefer to watch a match then you will find one at *Las Vegas Disc Golf Club* and they also organise the *Bag Tag Event (www.lvbagtag.com)*.

Eco travel in style

3

Small footprint The monorail takes holidaymakers from casino door to casino door in an environmentally friendly way, but there are also other stylish and sustainable ways of getting around in the city. The futuristic looking *Earth Limos* are not your usual gas-guzzlers. The chauffeurs take their guests from A to B in emission-free vehicles and in stylish luxury *(www.earthlimos.com, photo)*. Even better is the minimal environmental footprint of the *Yellow Checker Star* propane taxis *(www. ycstrans.com)* and the electric-powered *Segways (www.lasvegassegway.com* or *www. segwaylv.com)*.

18b – the place to be

Art 18b is the name for the Las Vegas neighbourhood which is the arts district where creative people have set up their studios and galleries. The ideal opportunity to get an overview of their events is when the artists open their doors on *First Friday Las Vegas*. Performance artists and musicians travel to this monthly event, and visitors are allowed to stroll through the studios. A map of all the participating locations can be viewed at *www. firstfriday-lasvegas.org*. The heart of the district is undoubtedly *The Arts Factory.* Although art pieces are not produced here, the centre hosts a variety of exhibitions – and a great bistro *(107 E. Charleston Blvd, photo).*

Rockabilly

Viva Las Vegas Feel like a little time travel? Then visit the largest Rockabilly event in the world: *Viva Las Vegas* is held every spring in the city and it is quite sensational. Festival goers all get dressed up in outfits from the 1950s. It is petticoats and beehives as far as the eye can see *(www. vivalasvegas.net, photo).* So that you don't stand out make an appointment with Lety, the hairdresser at *Curl Up n Dye (2550 S. Rainbow Blvd).* All that you need next is an outfit to match your hairstyle, and you can find that at *Betty Page Clothing.* Prominent fans of the clothing label include the singer Pink and the movie stars Penelope Cruz and Leighton Meester *(in Planet Hollywood).*

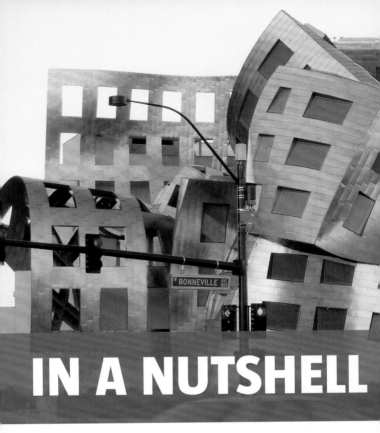

IN A NUTSHELL

ARCHITECTURE

Some of Las Vegas' original motels and businesses remain on Fremont and Main Street. The first themed hotel on the Strip was opened in 1966 and it went on to become very famous in Las Vegas: *Caesars Palace*. Back then this Roman fantasy world cost an astonishing 25 million dollars to build. The next big fantasy hotel was the *Mirage* (1989), followed by a dozen other themed hotels in the 1990s, which were inspired by cities like Paris and Venice, by the Middle Ages *(Excalibur)* or by the Egyptian pharaohs *(Luxor)*. Also brand new at the time was the concept of covering a whole street with a roof

and using it as a backdrop for light shows *(Fremont Street Experience)*. The groundbreaking concept is credited to Jon Jerdes. The new millennium casinos rely on ultra luxury like the *Wynn* or on stylish design like the *Aria* or the *Cosmopolitan,* which had cost 4 billion dollars to build.

But Las Vegas also offers exiting architecture apart from the casinos: like the *Lou Ruvo Center for Brain Health* built by Frank Gehry in 2010. A brain research centre, which in typical Gehry design, has an iconic landmark facade – comparable to the complex structures of the brain. Or just next to it, the chunky *World Market Center*, and the *Clark County Government*

Photo: Lou Ruvo Center for Brain Health

Musicians, speculators & millionaires: the entertainment metropolis offers a fertile ground for a multitude of different careers

Center which appears to be sinking into the desert. Many of the new buildings are LEED certified meaning that they are ecologically sustainable in design and suitable for the desert climates.

B LACK VEGAS

Musicians like Louis Armstrong, Nat King Cole and Sammy Davis Jr belonged to the most beloved entertainers in Las Vegas during the 1940s and 1950s. They had to enter the stage from the back door – because they were black. They were given paper cups instead of glasses, and were not allowed to move around freely in the casinos and restaurants. They were not even allowed to stay over in the hotels on the Strip. The *Moulin Rouge* opened in 1955, the first mainly black hotel casino. It immediately became a

Rien ne va plus – where the croupiers call the bets

huge hit, its shows instantly selling out. Yet, after only five months it was closed down and it is still uncertain to this very day why that happened. It is assumed that temptations and pressures from the casino owners on the Strip played a major role. Despite its early end, the Moulin Rouge and its star guests contributed to the emancipation of black people in Las Vegas and to the burgeoning civil rights movement in the USA.

ENERGY & WATER

Great weather is the only advantage that Las Vegas has going for it in its location in the desert. From an ecological point of view, temperatures of 40° C/ 104° F in the summer together with opulent swimming pools, are a nightmare. Thanks to the constantly whirring air-conditioners, Vegas homes and hotel rooms use double the amount of electricity than that of the average American home. A full 20 per cent of the total energy use of the city is used by the casinos,

some of them using as much energy as a small city – which is why most of them have their own generators in their cellars. Added to this is the constant water shortage. Nevada only receives four per cent of the Colorado River water, the rest goes to California and Arizona. During dry times, like the current spell that started in 2000, it becomes a real problem. In addition, Las Vegas alone uses 850 million kilowatt hours of electricity to pump its water from Lake Mead. This electricity is generated by coal-burning power plants – very bad for the environment.

In the past few years – out of economic necessity – there has been a change in attitude. The 150,000 hotel rooms have long since stopped using extravagant shower heads, they have been replaced with water-saving ones. All new buildings and casinos must comply with strict regulations and many, like the *Aria*, have been certified as green buildings. Even Las Vegas' famous neon signs now flash with energy-saving LED lights.

tels in Las Vegas, including the *MGM Grand*. His company also has a part in the new CityCenter.

Steve Wynn, the ex-owner of the *Golden Nugget*, had the *Mirage*, *Treasure Island* and the *Bellagio* built on the strip. His most expensive luxury casinos, the *Wynn Las Vegas* and *Encore,* were opened in 2005 and 2008. He himself never got into trouble with the law, but many of his co-workers had connections with the Mafia and his methods were not necessarily the most refined.

P AIUTE INDIANS

Before white settlers took over the land on which Las Vegas was built, it was inhabited by the Paiute, a nomadic Indian tribe. Within a few decades of the 19th century the Paiute were driven from the land by invading whites, and met their demise through disease and poverty. Today the remaining Paiute live off the sales of cigarettes and cigars, handmade woven baskets, jewellery and other handmade artefacts that can be bought at the *Las Vegas Paiute Commercial Plaza (1225 N. Main St)*. In 1995, *Snow Mountain*, the first golf resort on Paiute land was opened *(10325 Nu-Wav Kaiv Blvd)*.

I NVESTORS & SPECULATORS

Howard Hughes, one of the first major business men without ties to the Mafia, paved the way for public companies to operate casinos without each shareholder having to present a license. He was regarded as a headstrong, eccentric person with a thousand ailments, who would quarantine himself and his entourage in the luxury suites of the old *Desert Inn*. He quickly bought the place after the owner tried to get rid of him. During 1970, he left the city exactly in the same way that he came in – on a stretcher.

Kirk Kerkorian, the son of an Armenian immigrant – today one of the richest men in America – has had an amazing rags to riches career. He dropped out of school in the eighth grade and started doing odd jobs, learned to fly, did some dangerous flights for the British Royal Air Force and made name for himself in 1945 as a high roller. Apparently very lucky indeed, he won enough capital to build several ho-

P OLITICS

Politically, Nevada is divided up just like the other 49 US states: with a governor and the bicameral *Nevada Legislature* which has its seat in the capital, Carson City, in northern Nevada. The metropolis of Las Vegas is a bit more complex because the actual city only encompasses the old area around Fremont Street and the area north-west of it. The largest part of the Las Vegas Strip and its casinos actually belong to the town of Paradise, which like Las Vegas, lies in the governing district of Clark County. Many other small towns make up the metropolis. To avoid this confusion, many municipal facilities like the police or the *Marriage Licence Office* have been assigned to Clark County and are managed centrally.

PROSTITUTION

Although Las Vegas has a very different reputation: prostitution is actually illegal. Of course, this does not mean that there are no prostitutes. On the contrary: you can hardly walk along the Strip without some (mostly illegal immigrant) Latinos pressing their business cards – with naked girls and their telephone numbers – into your hands. Although the cards are designed to give a very personal touch, it is in fact highly organised pimping. Gone are the days when porters acted as go-betweens and procured girls and drugs and took a cut of the earnings. During the mid-1980s the police and prosecutors put an end to this system. Since then the rules of a free (underground) market apply, brothels in the area try to fill the gap in the market by sending fancy limousines to collect their clients, because prostitution is not illegal outside of Clark County.

SECURITY

Since the flighting of the film 'Ocean's Eleven', the whole world knows that there is a lot of money kept in Las Vegas and that big things happen there. But the reality is quite different, at least for the visitors. Because of the vast sums of money in circulation security measures are very tight and very sophisticated. There are cameras everywhere and security officers, who have the authority on casino property, can be seen everywhere. So you can actually feel very safe. However, Las Vegas is one of the US cities with the highest crime rate – about 10,000 violent crimes are committed annually. Widespread alcoholism, gambling, prostitution and drug use all contribute the crime statistics. Hopefully, you as visitor will not see this dark side of Las Vegas – as long as you stick to the usual unwritten rules. In the busy tourist area on the Strip, the dangers are limited. The biggest dangers here are not murders or robbery, but vehicle theft and drugs. So it is best not leave anything of value lying around in your car, and do not walk in dark side streets late at night, and stay away from drugs and 'working girls'.

TOUR OF GLITTERING LIGHTS

By day, Las Vegas can be a little boring. No neon glow, no bustling crowds, no attractions and so you will not find the usual sightseeing tours that you find in other cities. During the day, you can lounge around the swimming pool or take a trip to the Hoover Dam, by night you can set out to conquer the casinos. But should you like to know more about the history of the city, the five-hour Neon Lights Tour by *Gray Line Tours* can be recommended. The tour includes the major casinos and Fremont Street as well as a helicopter flight *(tel. 800 6 34 65 79 | www.grayline lasvegas.com)*. Las Vegas has all sorts of specialised tours: *Nite Tours (tel. 702 8 77 64 83 | www.nitetours.com)* for example, offers visits to three nightclubs by limousine – and no queuing at the door. At Bally's Casino, you can have a view of what happens backstage during a production with a tour titled, 'Jubilee! All Access Backstage Walking' *(tel. 702 9 67 49 38 | www.ballyslas vegas.com)*.

As vigilant as the pharaohs in the Luxor – security is very important in Las Vegas

THE RAT PACK

They were middle aged men but behaved like wild teenagers often spending the whole night drinking and partying with women. Yet, these guys – Frank Sinatra, Sammy Davis Jr, Dean Martin, Peter Lawford and Joey Bishop – always looked spick and span. Starched white collars, custom-made suits, the best eau de cologne and of course, a hat. From 1959, the Rat Pack wowed audiences every night in the *Sands,* which was later demolished to make room for the *Venetian,* until a fight between Sinatra and the casino owner ended the era in 1967. The musician even had close ties with John F. Kennedy. In a time of social and political conservatism, they brought life to the place and became legends – so much so that today tribute shows tell the stories of their era.

WAITERS & CROUPIERS

There are a few telecom and insurance companies in Las Vegas that provide work but almost 1.9 million people in the city are dependent on the gambling industry for employment: either directly, as dealers in the casinos and employees of the hotels or restaurants or indirectly as relatives, builders or teachers to the croupier's children. For them life in Las Vegas is just as it would be in any other suburb in America. But they have to carry the troubles of the gambling city with them: the high crime rate as well as the vagaries of the economy, when guests stay away and building projects are halted. That is exactly what happened during the crisis of 2008, from which the city has not yet recovered.

THE PERFECT DAY
Las Vegas in 24 hours

11:00am RELAX BY THE SWIMMING POOL

Las Vegas is deserted in the mornings so save your energy, sleep, spend a few hours next to the hotel swimming pool, enjoy a lazy breakfast or a lunch buffet in your own hotel or at a place like the *Mandalay Bay* → p. 54 on the southernmost end of the Strip.

01:00pm THE TITANIC OR THE MAFIA

Let's go: due to the afternoon heat, the best place to start is in the gigantic air-conditioned pyramid of the *Luxor* → p. 30 (tram from the Mandalay Bay). Depending on your interest, take an hour to discover sunken treasure in the Titanic exhibition, or go for the *Mob Experience* → p. 32 in the Tropicana's Mafia Experience Museum.

02:30pm ON THE STRIP

First take the tram from Luxor to the colourful castle of *Excalibur* → p. 30, then stroll along the Las Vegas Strip (photo left) to the north, past the Statue of Liberty in front of *New York New York* → p. 84, the luxury shopping centre *Crystals* → p. 65 and on to the *Bellagio* → p. 34 (shortened by tram from the Monte Carlo to the Bellagio). Do not miss the flower garden next to the Bellagio's lobby and the view of the water show in the lagoon. PS: and put a few dollars on the blackjack or roulette tables.

04:00pm TO CAESARS PALACE

On the northern side of Flamingo Road is *Caesars Palace* → p. 36 with its Roman theme and its ceiling of an artificial sky which covers the *Forum Shops* → p. 36 and 66. Now it is time to have sundowners and a snack: it may be cool in the mall, but the best place to be is on the terrace at *Serendipity 3* → p. 61 or across the way at the colourful *Margaritaville* → p. 71

05:30pm NEXT STOP IS VENICE

Opposite Caesars stroll through the *Flamingo* → p. 37, currently the oldest hotel on the Strip (photo right). Car buffs have to work an extra hour into their schedule to see the *Auto Collection at the Imperial Palace* → p. 34 next door. Next stop: *The Venetian* → p. 38 with an outside photo stop with gondolas and one inside on the first floor piazza.

Get to know some of the most dazzling, exciting and relaxing facets of Las Vegas – all in a single day

`07:00pm` PIRATES AND TIGERS

Check your watch: at 7pm and 8.30pm, across on the *Treasure Island* → p. 38 lagoon, the Amazons perform their show 'Sirens of TI' (free of charge) and you will get to see a ship sink on the Strip. Or, out of nostalgia or the love of animals, you can visit the Siegfried & Roy's white tigers in the *Mirage* → p. 37 next door.

`08:00pm` DOWNTOWN, THE OLD LAS VEGAS

Take a taxi or The Deuce bus Downtown and within 15 minutes you will be standing underneath the covered roof of the *Fremont Street Experience* → p. 42. After sunset the whole street lights up with fantastic light shows. Casinos worth seeing here are; the nostalgia-inspiring *Golden Gate* → p. 42, the *Golden Nugget* → p. 86 where you can swim with sharks, or the *Main Street Station* → p. 43 which is studded with small treasures and memorabilia from all over the world.

`09:30pm` BACK ON THE STRIP

Then it is back to the *Bellagio* → p. 34, where at night the water show with music is very romantic (until midnight). Around you the neon signs will be lit up and twinkling in all their glory (photo right). Stroll across to the *Paris* → p. 38, maybe back to *Caesars Palace* → p. 36 again, or go to the stylish The Cosmopolitan in the multi-floored nightclub, the *Marquee* → p. 71 for a cocktail.

`10:30pm` SHOWTIME

The last highlights of the day are Las Vegas' famous shows – a classic revue like *Jubilee!* → p. 76 in Bally's, or a Cirque du Soleil production like '*O*' → p. 77 at the Bellagio, or *Viva Elvis!* → p. 77 at the Aria. If you still have some energy left, it is time to try some *Gambling* → p. 88 until the early hours of the morning ...

The Strip trolley bus to the starting point
Bus stop: Mandalay Bay or by Las Vegas Monorail
Station stop: MGM Grand Station

SIGHTSEEING

CITY **WHERE TO START?**
Start: on the corner of **Las Vegas Blvd/Flamingo Rd (112 B–C4)** (*🗺 B8*) go north to Caesars Palace, (lit up at night), to the Flamingo and the Venetian with its St Mark's Square and gondolas, then south to the Bellagio's water show and through the CityCenter to the Statue of Liberty at New York New York. Car parks are behind the Flamingo and the Imperial Palace on the eastern side of the Strip. The Deuce, the city bus, stops at all the major casinos.

You will not find this at any other tourist destination: the main attractions are the hotels themselves.

The first hotel casinos, which came into being after the legalisation of gambling in Nevada, became attractions because of their magnificent interiors. Fremont Street and some hotels on the Strip still give you an idea of what the Strip must have been like in its heyday. The Flamingo or the Riviera, for example, as well as the somewhat ostentatious Tropicana, which has not escaped the influence of the latest trends completely – were all opened in the 1950s. The gigantic, themed hotels which opened in the 1980s and 1990s today

Photo: The CityCenter complex

Themed hotels as objects on display: in the city of artifice and replicas, the imagination has no limits

attract more than just the general gaming public. Replica versions of the Manhattan skyline, the Eiffel Tower and the Grand Canal: Las Vegas is the city of perfect fakes and fantasy copies.

If you believe that money kills the imagination – this city proves just the opposite. White tigers and hammerhead sharks, glittering neon lights three floors tall, roller coasters around the hotel, original paint-

ings by Picasso, Monet and Renoir, trapeze artists above the gambling tables, the Eiffel Tower and Lake Como in the middle of the desert – whoever thinks that they have seen it all, is in for a new surprise at the next casino. In all of the large hotels, you can easily spend days entertaining yourself and not wanting for anything. Every hotel offers dozens of shops, restaurants in all categories, beautiful and exotic

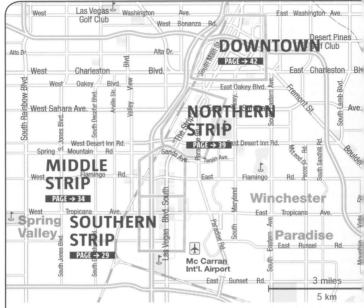

The map shows the location of the most interesting districts. There is a detailed map of each district on which each of the sights described is numbered.

landscaped gardens, fully equipped fitness centres, sometimes also tennis courts, exquisite wellness centres, massive swimming pools (unfortunately only for use of hotel guests, but you can at least have a look), bars, shows, and at least one special attraction. Higher, better, bigger, faster is this city's motto. No wonder then, that the most exciting entertainment rides and the most advanced Imax theatres are found here. The city also tries to keep up and be the best in the field of fine arts and you can see priceless works of art in the Bellagio Gallery of Fine Art, the Centaur Art Gallery and in the new CityCentre. They display art both from old masters as well as famed Americans like Andy Warhol, Roy Lichtenstein or Dale Chihuly.

Even the museums in Las Vegas are interesting – that is if you can find the time for them between the shows and all the sights – museums like the ecologically orientated Springs Preserve, for example, or good art exhibitions. To this end, casinos offer popular and perfectly executed exhibitions, displaying everything from the fate of the Titanic or an exciting and riveting interactive exhibition of the Mafia's connection to the city.

One of the most impressive things that Las Vegas has to offer, is the view from the city's ☀ observation towers, with the mountains and the desert in the far distance. A stunning contrast, especially with the slowly setting sun and the lights going on. Even though Las Vegas is the city of imitation, this is something you will not have seen or experienced before.

Most of the attractions are right on the Strip. Even though the hotels are right next to each other most of the casino facilities are so large, that a visit to one of the neighbouring buildings could turn into a rather long walk. Despite this, the best way to travel is simply to walk. First of all you will miss nothing and secondly you will almost always get stuck in traffic if you use any other means of transport (taxi, bus). A good alternative for longer distances is the monorail, although some stops are right at the back of the casinos (good for conference visitors).

Orientation: *Las Vegas Boulevard* runs almost vertically through the centre of the city. It is subdivided into *North* and *South.* The Strip is a part of the southern boulevard, which is why you will often see the address *Las Vegas Blvd S. (S. = South).* For clarity's sake, we have divided the 3.7 mile strip into three parts and describe Downtown and surrounds separately. The map shows the division of the interesting sections of the Strip and Downtown. You will find a map for each area with the attractions marked by a number.

SOUTHERN STRIP

The strip expands continuously, the southernmost mega-hotel is currently the Mandalay Bay. The area described here stretches from Russel Road in the south up to Harmon Avenue.

■1■ CITYCENTER ★ ⏱ (112 B5) (*∅ B9*)
This city within a city cost almost 10 billion dollars to build. It is the largest privately

MARCO POLO HIGHLIGHTS

financed project in America, which was opened by the MGM Mirage hotel group in 2010. The complex includes three hotels; the *Aria*, the *Vdara* and the *Mandarin Oriental* that collectively have almost 5000 hotel rooms, and also the luxurious *Crystals* shopping centre. Its roof is a spectacular faceted construction designed by the architect Daniel Libeskind. This building set the bar high for Las Vegas, as it was built according to the latest building criteria and therefore has its own nine megawatt power plant and is also highly efficient in water recycling and use. Aside from Crystals, another attraction is the INSIDER TIP *Cihuly Gallery* in front of the Aria, where some spectacular works of American glass artists are exhibited. An elevated railway connects the complex with the Monte Carlo and the Bellagio. *Las Vegas Blvd S/E Harmon Ave | www.citycenter.com*

Luxor – lights glowing in the pyramid interior

2 EXCALIBUR (114 A1) (*𝄞 B10*)

The medieval castle, which looks as though it has been built from paper maché, would have looked very strange to King Arthur. The blue, red and golden towers are probably the most kitsch buildings in the city. At twilight Excalibur's turrets are lit up and the illuminated building is quite a sight against a dark night sky. The ⚹ pedestrian bridge over the Strip and the Tropicana Avenue offers good views of the towers. The medieval themed and slightly shabby interior of the hotel is not necessarily worth a visit. *3850 Las Vegas Blvd S. | www.excalibur.com*

3 LUXOR ★ (114 A2) (*𝄞 B11*)

The glass pyramid, made up of 39,000 windows, is the fourth largest pyramid in the world. A ten-storey high sphinx guards the entrance to the hotel that has interior and exterior walls covered in authentic hieroglyphics. Inside, pharaohs sit (half as high as the originals but still huge), flanked by majestic lions and subtly lit ponds. A ride in one of the elevators is remarkable as it is adapted to the slant of the pyramid. Special attractions in the hotel are:

– INSIDER TIP *Titanic: The Artifact Exhibition:* At the time that it sank in the icy Atlantic in 1912, the Titanic was the largest cruise ship in the world. A lot of items have been recovered from the wreckage during several dives in the 1990s. The exhibition includes items like travel bags, jewellery, dishes and other personal belongings. Photos and reproductions, like the exact replica of the glamorous main stairs in its original size, are all poignant reminders of the tragedy that took place one hundred years ago *(daily 10am–10pm | entrance from $28)*.

– *Bodies ... The Exhibition:* Until recently this was the reserve of pathologists and doctors: a view into the human body. This

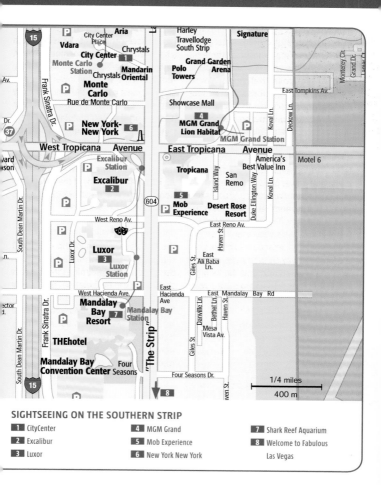

SIGHTSEEING ON THE SOUTHERN STRIP

1 CityCenter
2 Excalibur
3 Luxor
4 MGM Grand
5 Mob Experience
6 New York New York
7 Shark Reef Aquarium
8 Welcome to Fabulous Las Vegas

exhibition (that originated in China) provides a well prepared and detailed visual of all the body parts and organs *(daily 10am–10pm | entrance $32 | info tel. 702 2 62 44 44). 3900 S. Las Vegas Blvd | www. luxor.com*

4 MGM GRAND (112 C6) (*B–C10*)
One of the largest casinos in the city. It is divided into four thematic areas to

help you find your way. Although all in all the building is rather confusing. As you stroll through the mega resort you will come across new shopping streets and plazas everywhere. And there are always new attractions: a glass tunnel takes you through the glass enclosure of the ● *Lion Habitat* and allows you to see the lions from every angle, even from beneath (if you are lucky, one might just be on top of the tunnel). The lions work in shifts: six hours in the exhibition and then two days of freedom on a nearby ranch *(daily 11am–10pm | entrance free)*.

The *CSI* television series is the inspiration behind *CSI – The Experience*. As a visitor, you participate in an interactive challenge and you have to solve murders with high-tech methods at 15 different lab stations. You work with the forensic scientists, prepare and match DNA reports and examine bullet casings – be a crime scene investigator *(daily 10am–10pm | entrance $ 30 | www.csiexhibit.com). 3799 S. Las Vegas Blvd | www.mgmgrand.com*

5 MOB EXPERIENCE
(114 B1) (*M B–C10*)

The Mafia made Las Vegas great, after the Second World War, New York families of the Mob moved to the west and started to build the first casinos on the Las Vegas Strip. Those turbulent days can be experienced first-hand: the Mob Experience museum makes a gang member out of every visitor. Prove your money laundering skills at one of the 20 stations equipped with exciting high-tech adventure. Several descendants of Mafia families have donated heirlooms to the exhibition *(daily 10am–10pm | entrance $ 40 | www.lvme.com)*.

It is very fitting that the attraction is inside the *Tropicana Hotel*, as the casino resort (which was built in 1957) still had very close ties with the Mafia right up until the 1970s. When strolling through the (renovated) casino, you can still see some of the opulent tropical décor from its glory days. A major attraction is the Tiffany glass ceiling. *3801 Las Vegas Blvd S. | www.troplv.com*

6 NEW YORK NEW YORK ⭐
(112 B6) (*M B10*)

The casino hotel New York New York markets itself as the greatest city in Las Vegas. The *Empire State Building* (only 47 storeys high here) and eleven other famous skyscrapers build the perfect Manhattan skyline. Millions of visitors cross the Brooklyn Bridge in Las Vegas annually, while the original bridge over the East River (which is five times bigger)

THE LATEST TREND: OUTDOOR

Until the more recent past everything in Las Vegas happened indoors, because with temperatures of over 40° C/104° F during summer, there was no other choice. Thanks to air-conditioners, which constantly run at high speed, you do not need to worry about the weather in Las Vegas.

But suddenly the desert metropolis has discovered that for seven to eight months it actually has a very pleasant climate. Along the Strip, more and more outdoor venues have started popping up. The Wynn Las Vegas was the first casino to provide their restaurants with terraces, and now you can also dine outside at the Bellagio and the Paris.

The latest trend seems to be hotel rooms that have balconies, like those at the Signature and the newly built Cosmopolitan. Some casinos have nightclubs with terraces and some, like the Wynn of the Flamingo, even have outdoor gambling areas in their swimming pool areas.

only attracts 940,000 pedestrians. The Vegas replica of the *Statue of Liberty* even has its own island. The casino is a reproduction of *Central Park*. Other areas of the casino look like the *Rockefeller Centre*, bustling *Time Square* and the charming *Greenwich Village*.

The city even has typical graffiti on en-

⁊ SHARK REEF AQUARIUM
(114 A2) (⌖ B11)

In the shark glass tunnel you will get the feeling that you are swimming right amongst 2000 dangerous and endangered animals – including 15 different types of sharks. The aquarium is built like a sunken temple. *Sun–Thu 10am–8pm,*

Surrounded by sharks – Shark Reef Aquarium tunnel at the Mandalay Bay

trances to the stations and on the telephone booths. You will get the best view from the ☆ INSIDER TIP *gallery on the Grand Central Station side of the casino.* *The Roller Coaster*, which winds itself around the hotel complex, can be heard from inside the complex and sounds exactly like a train passing through a train station. Race around New York City's silhouette at 67mph. The Roller Coaster may be one of the older roller coaster rides in the city but it is not in the least bit boring *(Sun–Thu 11am–11pm, Fri–Sat 10.30am–midnight | entrance $14, day pass $25). 3790 S. Las Vegas Blvd | www.nynyhotelcasino. com*

Fri–Sat 10am–10pm | entrance $16.95 | in Mandalay Bay | 3950 S. Las Vegas Blvd | www.mandalaybay.com

⁸ WELCOME TO FABULOUS LAS VEGAS (114 B4) (⌖ B12)

A photo souvenir taken with the famous neon sign, 'Welcome to Fabulous Las Vegas' is a must. The 26ft high sign has welcomed visitors coming into Vegas on the old airport road since 1959. Aside from this sign, which is south of Mandalay Bay, there is another one – framed by palm trees – on the northern Strip at the corner of 4th Street (111 D4) (⌖ D3). *5100 Las Vegas Blvd S.*

MIDDLE STRIP

You need only to walk about a mile to get from the wonders of little Paris to the canals and squares of Venice. The section described here stretches from East Harmon Avenue up to Spring Mountain Road.

1 AUTO COLLECTIONS AT THE IMPERIAL PALACE ●
(112 C4) (*∅ B–C8*)

More than 300 vintage cars to view, admire or even buy. The displays change continuously and you can see the Cadillacs belonging to Al Capone (1930), and Marilyn Monroe (1959) and even the parade limousine (1952 Chrysler) that once belonged to US President Eisenhower. If you don't have enough money to buy yourself a 1914 dove blue Mercedes ($550,000), then there is always something like the 1965 VW Beetle convertible for about $15,500. An exhibition not just for car lovers! *Daily 10am–6pm | entrance $8.95 , free entrance with printed coupon from the website | in the Imperial Palace | 3535 S. Las Vegas Blvd | www.autocollections.com*

2 BELLAGIO ★
(112 B4–5) (*∅ B9*)

Romantic, elegant and plush: this is one of the most attractive luxury hotels on the Boulevard. From the outside it looks like an idyllic Italian village on Lake Como, and of course it even has its own lake. Every afternoon and evening, the water fountains of the lake dance a ● *water ballet* accompanied by melodies from Broadway shows, famous operas or Frank Sinatra *(every 30 minutes in the afternoons, at night every 15 minutes)*. ✹ INSIDER TIP ▶ Get the best view from the Eiffel Tower on the opposite side.

Vintage car in the Auto Collections at the Imperial Palace

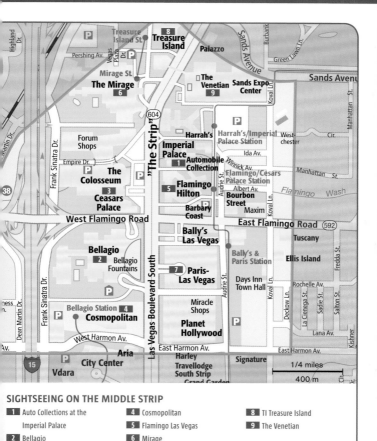

SIGHTSEEING ON THE MIDDLE STRIP

1 Auto Collections at the Imperial Palace
2 Bellagio
3 Caesars Palace
4 Cosmopolitan
5 Flamingo Las Vegas
6 Mirage
7 Paris Las Vegas
8 TI Treasure Island
9 The Venetian

The Italian elegance is continued in the interior: arches, columns and marble. Even the slot machines are covered in fabric to look little more elegant. The foyer's ceiling is a decorated bouquet of glass flowers, made out of more than 2,000 pieces by the American artist Dale Chiluly. Take a stroll through the botanical garden, where thousands of plants are beautifully arranged, the arrangements depend on the seasons and you should also take a look at the INSIDER TIP Mediterranean swimming pool which can be seen from the public terrace.

Inside the Bellagio the *Gallery of Fine Art* shows fine temporary exhibitions in elegant rooms with masterpieces by Andy Warhol and Claude Monet on loan from the *Boston Museum of Fine Art*. Tickets are in high demand so it is best to buy them

Do as the ancient Romans – the swimming pool at Caesars Palace

luxury in the style of the ancient Romans. The most attractive part of the hotel, which opened in 1966, is the extraordinary shopping centre, the *Forum Shops*, which are spanned by an artificial sky where the sun rises and sets, clouds go by and stars shine at night. The days (and nights) pass quicker here than anywhere else.

The gods come to life in *Caesars Forum*: Bacchus, Venus, Apollo and Pluto debate about ancient Rome in the *Festival Fountain Show*. While in the new part of the mall (in the section where Poseidon stands vigil) a winged beast watches the *Fall of Atlantis Fountain Show* and the demise of the fabled island *(both shows on the hour, every hour, Sun–Thu 10am–11pm, Fri/Sat 10am–midnight | free entrance)*. The new entertainment centre, *Linq* is under construction outside of the hotel. The top attraction of the centre will be the largest roller coaster in the world at a height of 550ft.

Also situated at Caesars Palace, is the *Neil Leifer Gallery* where dynamic action photographs of celebrity sports stars are exhibited and sold by the New York photographer Neil Leifer *(daily 1pm–9pm | free entrance). 3570 S. Las Vegas Blvd | www.caesarspalace.com*

■4 COSMOPOLITAN
(112 B5) (*ΩJ B9*)

One of the newest casino palaces. When their financing fell flat shortly before the completion of the casino, a German bank rescued the project and took over the financing – because they believed in it as an investment – and they thus became the owners of an American casino. Although there is no one main attraction it is still worth strolling through the multi-floored, stylish foyer with its gigantic lights, innovative shops and restaurants on the upper floors. Excellent buffet restaurant. Also very beautiful from the

in advance *(daily 10am–6pm, Wed, Fri/Sat until 7pm | entrance $15 | guided tours daily from 2pm). 3600 S. Las Vegas Blvd | tel. 702 6 93 71 11 | www.bellagio.com*

■3 CAESARS PALACE
(112 B4) (*ΩJ B8*)

Tall slender cypresses, Roman temples, fountains and busts, arches and columns –

swimming pool deck with a view over the Strip. For relaxation the hotel offers the unusually designed ● *Sahra Spa & Hammam* and elegant massage rooms. *3708 Las Vegas Blvd S. | www.cosmopolitan lasvegas.com*

5 FLAMINGO LAS VEGAS
(112 C4) (*ⅅ B–C8*)

Mobster Bugsy Siegel built the first hotel on the Strip in the middle of the desert in 1946, at the time it was so luxurious and extravagant that even the cleaning staff wore tuxedos. Although there is not even one stone left of the original building, the flashing neon signs show that this casino has not made the leap to a more modern, themed hotel. It has a lovely *Wildlife Habitat* with lush pine trees, palm trees and magnolias and a menagerie of exotic birds: pheasants, herons, ibises, parrots, penguins and of course flamingos. *Daily 24 hours | free entrance | 3555 S. Las Vegas Blvd | www.flamingolasvegas.com*

6 MIRAGE
(112 B3) (*ⅅ B7–8*)

This casino is believed by some to have triggered the hotel building boom in the desert during the 1990s. It does appear as a mirage in the desert and its landscaped gardens – palm trees, banana trees, orchids and a lagoon with waterfalls – shields the hotel from the busy Strip. Every night you can watch a volcano eruption *(7pm– 11pm on the hour)*. In 1989 the volcano was the first main attraction on the Strip and in 2009 it was further transformed into a high-tech show with lots of pyrotechnics. The eruption also has a dramatic music score with drum arrangements by the Grateful Dead drummer Mickey Hart.

In the foyer it feels as if you are somewhere in the South Seas. Behind the reception desk is a fish tank with thousands of colourful fish swimming around a coral reef. The thick glass sheets of the aquarium hold back about 21,100 US gallons of water. Underneath a glass dome is a small tropical rainforest with palm and banana trees. Outside in ● *Siegfried & Roy's Secret Garden* you can admire the magnificent white cats, one of which injured its master Roy Horn quite badly in 2003. In the neighbouring *Dolphin Habitat* you can play ball with the dolphins. *Daily*

LOW BUDGET

▶ Browse through the events magazines like 'What's on?' *(www. whats-on.com)* or 'Vegas Magazine' *(lasvegasmagazine.com)* for coupons. There are even coupon websites available like *www.vegascoupons. com*, or you can find special promotion codes on the Internet, for example at *www.smartervegas.com*. Even restaurants, shows and exhibitions use coupons in their marketing. You can get two tickets for the price of one, or a free starter or even a free main dish.

▶ Free shuttle buses travel to almost all the hotel casinos and other attractions that are away from the Strip, e.g. to the Orleans, the Hard Rock Hotel or the Rio Suites. The monorails between the Bellagio, CityCenter and Monte Carlo, between Mirage and the TI Treasure Island as well as the line between Excalibur–Luxor– Mandalay Bay are all for free.

▶ Visit the *www.vegasfreebie.com* website for an overview of the free attractions and shows in Las Vegas.

11am–6.30pm, Sat/Sun from 10am | entrance $17 | 3400 S. Las Vegas Blvd | www.mirage.com

7 PARIS LAS VEGAS ★
(112 C4–5) (𝄞 B–C9)

'Bonjour Messieurs!' The staff here greet their guests in their best high school French. Inside and out this miniature ver-

Paris Las Vegas: the unmistakable Eiffel Tower

sion of the City of Lights, invites you to explore the meticulously detailed replica of the *Arc de Triomphe* or take a walk on the *Rue de la Paix*. Except for their size, the facades of the *Louvre*, the opera house and the town hall all look exactly like the Parisian originals. The replica of the *Eiffel Tower* is exactly half the size of the French one and was built using the original 1887 plans. Glass lifts take you to the 🔆 *viewing platform*, where the glittering city lies at your feet *(daily from 9.30am–12.30am | entrance $7.50–22). 3655 S. Las Vegas Blvd | www.parislasvegas.com*

8 TI TREASURE ISLAND
(112 C3) (𝄞 B7)

The pirate themed Treasure Island is trying to update their image and in the lagoon in front of the casino the pirates now have to take the island back from scantily clad sirens. Working on the premise that sex sells, the revamped free 20 minute show ★ ● *The Sirens of TI,* is now far raunchier. A rather dubious improvement but still worth a visit to see the acrobatics and pyrotechnics played out against the night sky. It is not that often that you get the opportunity to experience a ship sinking right in front of you. As soon as the audience starts to leave, the ship reappears again *(daily at dusk from 5.30pm, 7pm, 8.30pm, 10pm, during summer also 11.30pm | in the Sirens' Cove in front of the TI Treasure Island). 3300 S. Las Vegas Blvd | www.treasureislandlasvegas.com*

9 THE VENETIAN ★
(112 C3) (𝄞 C7–8)

St Mark's Square, the *Doge's Palace*, the *Campanile* and the *Grand Canal* – everything just as it is in Venice (well, almost) and statues, mosaics, and tiles that match their originals down to the finest detail. Security staff wear the uniforms of the Venetian police and gondoliers ferry their passengers from one shore to the other *(Sun–Thu 10am–11pm, Fri/Sat 10am–midnight | price $16 | duration: approx. 15min, same day reservations recommended | tel. 702 4 14 43 00).*

On St Mark's Square, costumed opera

singers belt out arias, artists juggle while living statues only blink their eyelashes every now and then *(varying time schedule for the shows)*. The only thing missing is Venice's uniquely musty smell. A world away from that are the wax models in *Madame Tussauds*. If you have ever wanted to dance with Britney Spears, party with Julia Roberts and Brad Pitt, have a photo taken with Mick Jagger and Madonna, or wanted to see Neil Armstrong and George W. Bush, then this is the right place for you. There are over 100 celebrities waiting in the wax museum. Some of the actors look quite good. Jodie Foster and George Clooney, for example, look deceptively real but some of the musician (like Mick Jagger and Michael Jackson) appear unreal and a possibly even little ill! At the end of the exhibition you can see the process involved in the making of the wax figures. *Daily from 10am | entrance $25 (far too expensive, but many brochures offer coupons) | 3355 S. Las Vegas Blvd | www.venetian.com*

NORTHERN STRIP

The Stratosphere Tower is right at the end of the northern Strip. This part of the Strip boasts a circus world, a water park and the new Wynn Las Vegas. The northern Strip described here, stretches from Spring Mountain Road up to the Stratosphere Hotel.

◾1◾ RIVIERA (113 D1) (*ɱ C–D6*)

The 1955 'The Riv' was one of the first casinos on the Strip that was built with a tower for the rooms. Before that the hotels were all built like big motels. During the early days, the Riviera was popular in Mafia circles and later made an appearance in many Hollywood movies. Even if the Riviera's heyday is over, the casino is still great as a film set and it still embodies the 'old' Vegas. *2901 S. Las Vegas Blvd | www.rivierahotel.com*

Venetian gondolas, great art and wax figures – the Venetian has a lot to offer

2 STRATOSPHERE
(111 D5) ( D4)

The so-called 'needle', is the highest building west of the Mississippi, it is five blocks (and the blocks are long on the Strip) away from the other attractions on the Boulevard. But the Stratosphere is worth the effort of a bus ride or a walk and paying the $16 entrance fee *(Sun–Thu 10am–1pm, Fri/Sat 10am–2pm)* for the view from the 1148ft high ★ ● ⚡ *observa-*

The Stratosphere's 164ft free fall plunge

tion decks on the 108th floor. Despite its distance from the Strip, its super view and three nerve-racking rides make the hotel attractive and it does manage to attract visitors. One of the rides is *Insanity – The Ride* where an octopus-like chain carousel takes you over the edge of the tower and then spins you through the air. *Big Shot* carries you 164ft up in the air in just 2.5 seconds, only to let you (almost) free fall downwards. If you dare to open your eyes, the view from up here is great! The third attraction *X Scream*, is 885ft high and takes you over the edge of the tower at 30mph *(Sun–Thu 10am–1am, Fri/Sat 10am–2am | ride $13, incl. viewing tower $22, all rides incl. viewing tower $31)*.

Those looking for the ultimate thrill can even jump over the edge of the tower platform. The jump is controlled by a steel cable which stops you before impact. The *Skyjump* is what this controlled form of insanity is called and costs $99 *(Sun–Thu 11am–1am, Fri/Sat 11am–2am). 2000 S. Las Vegas Blvd | www.stratospherehotel. com*

3 WYNN/ENCORE (112 C2) ( C7)

Steve Wynn clearly wanted to establish a monument to himself with this luxurious building. The Wynn is protected from the crowds on the Strip by a 131ft high mountain. Curtain waterfalls tumble down into the *Lake of Dreams* and a forest of tall Aleppo pine trees provide shade. The interior has lots of marble, gold (or the colour gold at least) and exquisite carpets. Both the Wynn and neighbouring Encore, which opened in 2008, do not have any theme in the traditional sense however they both aim to embody an overwhelming sense of wealth and elegance. Similar to Wynn's Bellagio, but even more opulent and more elegant. In the shopping area you will only find designer shops with prices that will make your eyes water.

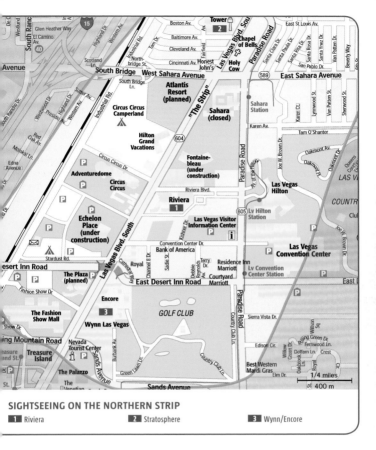

SIGHTSEEING ON THE NORTHERN STRIP

1 Riviera **2** Stratosphere **3** Wynn/Encore

Even if you do not want to spend $500 on a pair of shoes, you should still take a browse and see the beautiful footwear the *Shoein* has to offer.

From the *Country Club*, you have views of the soft, lush lawns of the well-designed golf course. Some of the cafés and restaurants (not all of them are that expensive) have ☆ terraces on the lake *(closed during summer due to the heat)*. After dusk you will have the best view of the light show, which is shown throughout

the night in different sequences *(free entrance)*.

Steve Wynn, who has always been a Ferrari fan, has given the Italian car manufacturers a monument in his hotel: *Penske Wynn Ferrari Maserati*, a showroom with almost a dozen rare Ferraris, none of them priced below $700,000. Visitors come daily to admire these valuable rarities *(Mon–Sat 9am–6pm | entrance $10)*. 3131 S. Las Vegas Blvd | tel. 702 7 70 70 00 | www. wynnlasvegas.com

DOWNTOWN

The former city centre – a bit run-down after visitors started concentrating on the Strip – has been spruced up again during the past few years. Despite all the efforts: the glitter does not seem as grand and the pomp and splendour seem a little transient. It is also more noticeable because the streets are surrounded by shabby, unsafe neighbourhoods. But not to worry, Fremont Street itself holds no danger. The Deuce bus will take you to the Downtown area.

provides warmth in the winter. The canopy is covered with over 12 million LED lights and fitted with a sound system that can compete with any arena concert system. The nightly *Sky Parade*, a high-tech laser show with music, is a real experience *(starting at the onset of darkness until midnight, each show is an hour)*.

Because everybody missed the shabby appeal of the old *Glitter Gulch*, the *Initiative Neon Museum* has started to restore the classic old neon lights of Las Vegas and set them up as an outdoor gallery along the promenade. Take a look at the oversized cowboy created in 1967 which now

Downtown's spectacular high tech light show – the Fremont Street Experience

■1■ FREMONT STREET EXPERIENCE ★ ●
(111 E1–2) (∅ E1)

This pedestrian zone – four blocks long – is a cheap alternative to the Strip. It is very popular (especially at night) for its street cafés, shops and the electronic canopy which cools the streets down during the impossibly hot summer days and

decorates the entrance to the pedestrian zone. *Between Las Vegas Blvd and Main St | www.vegasexperience.com*

■2■ INSIDER TIP GOLDEN GATE
(111 E1) (∅ E1)

Built almost hundred years ago, this is therefore the oldest hotel and casino on

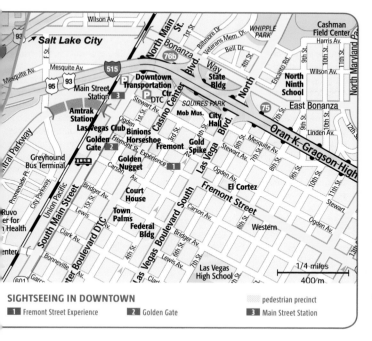

SIGHTSEEING IN DOWNTOWN

1 Fremont Street Experience   2 Golden Gate   3 Main Street Station

////// pedestrian precinct

Fremont Street. Much of the original wood panelling has remained intact. Restored in the style of San Francisco in the 1930s. Would you like a taste of what it was like in the casinos some 50 or 70 years ago? Here you can taste the atmosphere! *1 Fremont St | www.goldengate casino.net*

3 INSIDER TIP **MAIN STREET STATION**
(111 E1) (*E1*)

Antique collectables from all over the world give this hotel the feeling of a small museum: a chandelier from the Paris Opera House, street lamps from Brussels, a fireplace from a Scottish castle and a piece of the Berlin wall (in the gent's toilet). There are also a number of items from the Wild West era at the beginning of the 20th century: wood panelling, wooden

benches, and ornately decorated cash registers behind bars. *200 N. Main St | www.mainstreetcasino.com*

AWAY FROM THE STRIP

The further away from the Strip, the harder it is for the casinos to attract the attention of tourists and that is why the casinos here usually resort to luring their clientele with very reasonable prices. Of course there are exceptions and there are those, like the Hard Rock Hotel – which is hardly cheap – that try very hard to make themselves special. Some attractions are easily accessible by bus, others only by taxi. But you can be certain

that the tips mentioned here will make the trip worthwhile.

INSIDER TIP ▶ **ATOMIC TESTING MUSEUM** (113 E4) (*ffl E8*)

The history of atomic testing in Nevada, which was suspended in 1992, is shown through photos, artefacts and reports by former employees. *Mon–Sat 10am–5pm, Sun noon–5pm | entrance $12 | 755 E. Flamingo Rd | www.atomictesting museum.org | bus 202 East from corner of Strip/Flamingo Rd*

GUN STORE (116 C4) (*ffl H10*)

Don't forget you are in the Wild West! But even that has changed over the years. In the Gun Store, target practice is no longer done on targets of horse thieves but instead they use the image of Osama bin Laden. You can try your hand at shooting anything from a Beretta to a machine gun here. For many Americans handling a gun is something quite normal but for most foreign tourists it is rather a bizarre experience, certainly one that they are not allowed to do at home. *Daily 9am–6.30pm | price according to weapon starting at $10 plus ammunition | 2900 E. Tropicana Ave | www.thegunstorelasvegas. com | bus 201 East from corner of Strip/Tropicana Ave*

MARJORIE BARRICK MUSEUM (113 F5) (*ffl E–F9*)

Study the country and its people: Mexican folk art from the 19th century, Indian pottery and prehistoric objects from the whole south-west of the USA and South America. Also on display are any and everything that crawls and flies: snakes, iguanas and tortoises, spiders and cockroaches. The museum's garden proves how beautiful and varied desert plants can be. *Mon–Fri 8am–4.45pm, Sat 10am–2pm | entrance $5 | on the campus of the UNLV (University of Nevada at Las Vegas) | 4505 Maryland Parkway | barrickmuseum.unlv.edu | bus 201 East from the corner of Strip/Tropicana Ave*

MOB MUSEUM (111 E1) (*ffl E1*)

The Mafia has never left Vegas: the city's latest museum, which opened 2012, shows the rise and fall of the Mob with many documents and interactive exhibitions. The setting is ironically the former court house on the edge of Downtown, where some real Mafia attacks took place. *300 Stewart Ave | www.themobmuseum.org*

RELAX & ENJOY

▶ After a long night of gambling, nothing feels better than a massage, so the casino hotels lure visitors with their super large, lavish spa areas. In the ultra modern *Aria Spa (3730 Las Vegas Blvd S. (112 B5) (ffl B9) | tel. 702 5 90 77 57)* which is decorated with lots of wood and stone, you can have a hot stone massage and then rest in a salt-infused room. In the elegant ● *Bellagio Spa (3600 Las Vegas Blvd S. (112 B4) (ffl B9) | tel. 702 6 93 74 72)* experience a Watsu water massage or have your own personal fitness trainer. Besides having Ayurveda massage rooms and saunas, the massive ● *Canyon Ranch Spa (in the Venetian | 3355 Las Vegas Blvd S. (112 C3) (ffl C7–8) | tel. 702 4 14 36 00)* also has its own spa restaurant and a fitness club with climbing walls which is bound to get you fighting fit for your next evening out on the town ...

Old neon signs that have found a new home at the Neon Museum

INSIDER TIP ▶ NEON MUSEUM
(116 C3) (*∅ O*)

Where do the old casinos and motels signs go when they have come to the end of their use? To the Neon Boneyard. Some signs are restored and used again Downtown, but most have their final resting place here. The collection of over 100 faded, but historical signs are a great subject for amateur photographers and nostalgics. Guided tours only by appointment. *Entrance $15 | 821 Las Vegas Blvd N. | tel. 702 3 87 63 66 | www.neonmuseum.org | bus 113/ MAX*

NEVADA STATE MUSEUM
(116 B3) (*∅ O*)

Pioneer wagons, dinosaurs, casino chips – the lavish new building which opened in 2011 – houses exhibitions ranging from the history of the gambling city to the nature and wildlife of the region. Combine it with a visit to the neighbouring *Springs Preserve. Fri–Mon 10am–6pm | entrance* $10 | 309 Valley View Blvd | museums. nevadaculture.org | from the Strip bus 201, 202 or 204 West, then towards Valley View Blvd with bus 104 North*

INSIDER TIP ▶ SPRINGS PRESERVE ☺
(116 B3) (*∅ O*)

Las Vegas was founded right here at this spring but the water dried up in 1962. The Springs Preserve is a nature-based museum which shows the beauty of the desert, a historic overview of the city's early days and ideas for the environmentally conscious. More than 100 exhibitions in five buildings (amongst them an energy-saving kitchen), as well as nature trails, concerts in the amphitheatre, video games and a flood demonstration that flushes thousands of gallons of recycled water into a gorge every 20 minutes. The *Springs Café* serves healthy dishes by celebrity chef Wolfgang Puck and there is a concert every Thursday. *Daily 10am–6pm | entrance $18.95 | 333 S. Valley View Blvd | www.*

Take a flight and experience the immense vastness and splendour of the Grand Canyon

springspreserve.org | from the Strip bus 201, 202 or 204 West, then towards Valley View Blvd with bus 104 North

THE RIO (112 A4) (𝄞 A8)

The Brazilian themed Rio, is situated about a mile west of the Strip. The two colourful glass towers are especially attractive at night. Inside, carnival is celebrated all year round. The much hyped stage of the *Masquerade Show in the Sky* has a carnival float suspended from the ceiling above the casino so the dancers strut their stuff above the crowd. Visitors are invited to change into costumes and dance along. But don't think that they will pay you to do so: a prime spot on a float will cost you $12.95. Apart from that, the show is free and the INSIDER TIP best view is from the second floor of the *Masquerade Village*! *Shows Thu–Sun 7pm–midnight | no entrance fee | 3700 W. Flamingo Rd | www.riolasvegas.com | bus 202 West from corner of Strip/Flamingo Rd*

TRIPS & TOURS

BOOTLEG CANYON FLIGHTLINES (117 D4) (𝄞 O)

Experience the famous canyon in a completely different way: steel cables take you at thrilling speeds across the desolate canyon. It is called zip lining and it will certainly give you an adrenalin rush. *Collection from Excalibur (114 A1) (𝄞 B10) | price $150 | Boulder City | tel. 702 2 93 68 85 | www.bcflightlines.com*

INSIDER TIP EXTRATERRESTRIAL HIGHWAY (116 A1) (𝄞 O)

The Alien landing strip! According to UFO experts more unknown flying objects are spotted along this section of State Route 375 than anywhere else in the world. It is about 125mi from Las Vegas (across Highway 93) and the road runs along the top secret Area 51, where the US Army tests top secret aeroplanes and apparently also tries to contact aliens. Even sceptics will find that the trip out there is a desert experience that is 'out of this world'.

GRAND CANYON ⭐ ☼
(116 B–C1) *(⬛ O)*

Las Vegas is said to be the doorway to the Grand Canyon but this is quite hard for foreign tourists to understand because the distances are really rather extreme: it is almost 250mi from the Strip to the world famous gorge. Bus tours to the canyon take very long, but there are a selection of flight companies that offer 'flight-seeing tours'. The Grand Canyon is 280mi long, 9mi wide and about 1mi deep – an impressive natural wonder. At dawn and twilight the view of the massive gorge with its brown, red and violet tinted light is an unforgettable experience. The *South Rim* inside of the National Park is open all year round, the *North Rim* only from mid May to mid October. The *West Rim*, which is closer to Las Vegas, is favoured by helicopter tours, and there is also the *Skywalk*, a gigantic free floating glass bridge that extends over the gorge in a horseshoe shape that is 4000ft above

the canyon *(daily 8am–5pm | info at www. grandcanyonskywalk.com)*.

Take note that the relatively expensive entrance fee for the bridge is included in tour prices, but if you come by rental car, you have to pay a reserve levy, parking, shuttle bus and a bridge levy – about $60–80. Brochures for the flight tours can be obtained from hotels. Within three hours (including transport from the hotel to the airfield) you could have seen everything: the West Rim of the Grand Canyon, *Lake Mead* and the *Hoover Dam.*

Other tours fly over the canyon from the east and, many also include hikes and lunch buffets as well as views of Indian villages. You will be underway for seven to eight hours. While aeroplanes can only take you over the canyon, helicopters can take you directly into the gorge – for more money of course – prices are seldom under $300 per person. Bus tours are the least fun: eight hours crammed into a bus and only two hours two view the canyon.

HOOVER DAM
(117 D4) *(⬛ O)*

The famous dam on the Colorado River lies just 37mi south-east of Las Vegas. It

JEEP OR HELICOPTER?

Whether it is for a few hours or a couple of days, many operators offer guided tours to areas surrounding Las Vegas and the Grand Canyon: by aeroplane, helicopter, bus or Jeep. Be sure to enquire about the exact duration and service offered (e.g. transport to the hotel, meals etc.). Also ask about special offers and about the total price (total including tax and other charges)!

Here are a few websites and operators to give you an overview:
– *Papillon Grand Canyon Helicopters (tel. 1 888 6 35 72 72 | www.papillon.com)*
– *Maverick Helicopters (tel. 1 888 2 61 44 14 | www.maverickhelicopter.com)*
– *Grand Canyon Tour Company (tel. 1 800 2 22 69 66 | www.grand canyontours.com)*
– *Pink Jeep Tours (tel. 1 888 9 00 44 80 | www.pinkjeep.com)*

The gigantic concrete retaining wall is 725ft high and almost as wide at the bottom. It was built between 1931 and 1936, to dam the Colorado River and supply water to the desert and to generate electricity. 5000 workers slaved day and night under very hard conditions: heat, dust, rock falls – and all of this at extreme heights. During the construction, 96 workers lost their lives. Today almost a half a million homes – and of course the neon lights of Las Vegas – get their electricity from the dam, named after the 31st US president, Herbert Hoover. But the majority of the electricity goes to California.

Coming from Las Vegas turn off on the access road to the Hoover Dam shortly after Boulder City, park in the large car park *($7)* and from there go to the *Visitor Centre,* where photos, videos and exhibitions display the history of the dam. On a guided tour, you will be able to see the dam's massive generators and take a lift to its base *(daily 9am–6pm, in winter until 5pm; in summer add on queuing time | entrance and guided tours $8–30 | www. usbr.gov/lc/hooverdam).*

In 2011 a new highway bridge spanning the Colorado River at the Hoover Dam, was opened. At the parking place at the access road you can get out and take an ● impressive photo of the bridge. Be aware that you are not allowed to stop while crossing the bridge!

On the drive back, take a detour from the US 93 on Lakeshore Drive to the north. Side streets lead you down to the shores of *Lake Mead*, its deep blue water in the centre of the brown desert mountains is quite a tranquil sight *(entrance to the Lake Mead National Recreation Area $10 per car | www.nps.gov/lame).* Swimming at *Boulder Beach* in the summer heat is wonderfully refreshing. Take your swimming gear with you, as well as provisions for a picnic at the lake! Even better is a swim

Bridge over the Colorado River

is easy to get to with a rented car, take Highway I 115 South-east, in the direction of Boulder City which changes to US 93/95 South. Guided tours are also on offer and can be booked from your hotel concierge at short notice.

at ● INSIDER TIP ▶ *Willow Beach* on the Colorado River with its lovely sandy beach and hire boats, just 12mi south-east of the Hoover Dam on Highway 93.

Lake Mead Cruises paddle steamer takes you across the lake and close to the dam wall and can be combined with dinner on board *(departure Lake Mead Marina at the Lakeshore Scenic Drive | fare $24–49, reservations essential during summer | tel. 702 2 93 61 80 | www. lakemeadcruises. com).*

RED ROCK CANYON
(0) (🛱 0)

Only a half an hour from the Strip, rugged red cliffs, Indian petroglyphs, Joshua trees and the silence of the Mojave Desert reserve await you. The reserve covers almost 200,000 acres and to get their you need to travel 18mi on the Charleston Blvd (US 159) west from the Strip, which will take you to the 💢 *Scenic Drive (during summer 6am–8pm, during winter until 5pm | entrance $7 per vehicle).* Numerous short hiking trails (like for example the *Calico Hills* trail) lead off from the almost 12.5mi long scenic road. Great in the heat of summer: the *Ice Box Canyon* with its waterfall.

The rich fiery red, grey and violet of the sandstone and limestone are at their most intense during dusk and dawn. A few minutes drive onwards on Highway 159, and you will find the INSIDER TIP ▶ *Spring Mountain Ranch (daily 10am–4pm | entrance $9 per vehicle | picnic sites | www.parks.nv.gov/smr.htm).*

This old Wild West ranch belonged to Vera Krupp, a German industrialists' widow, during the 1960s, she in turn sold it to the billionaire Howard Hughes. A tour through the main house (which still has some of its original furnishings) shows some of the more bizarre aspects of Las Vegas' history.

If you have forgotten to take your drinks, you will find relief after about a mile at the *Bonnie Springs Ranch*, a former cattle ranch. Here they not only have a lovely saloon with swing doors but also a restaurant. The whole ranch and the small Wild West town of *Old Nevada* are both unfortunately somewhat run down. During weekends they have shootouts and the villain is then hanged, of course it is always the same villain. *(Tue–Fri 10.30am–5pm Sat/Sun until 6pm | entrance $7, Sat/Sun $9 | www.bonniesprings.com).*

VALLEY OF FIRE STATE PARK ●
(117 D–E 1–2) (🛱 0)

This valley of fiery red sandstone and beautiful desert landscape is on the outskirts of Las Vegas and is about an hour away by car. First you head north on the Interstate I 15/US 93, then take the exit 75 of Highway 169 to the *Visitor Centre (daily 8.30am–4.30pm | entrance $10 per car | www.parks.nv.gov/vf.htm).* You can buy maps for walking trails and for attractions like the *Elephant Rock,* the *Seven Sisters* and ancient Indian petroglyphs. Over millennia the sun, water and the desert wind have carved out bizarre formations in the red sandstone of the valley. Be on the lookout for wild horses and donkeys, big horned sheep and desert tortoises.

Highway 169 winds along to the east to *Lake Mead* and to 💢 *Overton Beach*, about 7 miles. Here you will have a lovely view of the lake and the Virgin Mountains in the background. The *Lost City Museum (Thu–Sun 8.30am–4.30pm | entrance $5)* in the little village of *Overton* exhibits ceramics and other artefacts from the early Anzasazi culture. From here it is not far to the *Overton Arm* of Lake Mead, where you can swim during summer. Don't forget your lunch provisions and above all, remember to take water along!

FOOD & DRINK

Las Vegas is a gourmet's delight that is now well worth the trip. Once famous for its cheap buffets, the gambling city experienced a culinary revolution during the 1990s.

Suddenly the city became a magnet for top international chefs that started to arrive from all over the world. The Austrian Wolfgang Puck started the ball rolling when he opened *Spago* in 1992. Since then Puck has opened more than half a dozen restaurants in Las Vegas and many famous international chefs have followed suit since then.

One chef, André Rochat, has had a real rags to riches career: in 1965 he left

France with nothing to his name and headed to the USA. Today he owns two top restaurants (*André's* in the Monte Carlo and *Alizé* in the Palms) and is regarded as one of the world's top chefs. With the arrival of award-winning French chefs like Joël Robuchon and Alain Ducasse, Las Vegas established itself as a gourmet metropolis.

Since then, more and more American star chefs from other cities have also opened their own restaurants in Las Vegas: Michael Mina from San Francisco, Thomas Keller from the Napa Valley, Emeril Lagasse from New Orleans, Charlie Palmer from New York and many more.

Photo: Beijing Noodle No. 9

Elegant restaurants and inexpensive gourmet buffets: Las Vegas is a culinary metropolis with fine cuisine from all around the world

Whether it be foie gras or a juicy steak, sweet and sour pork or sushi, enchiladas, cannelloni or other exotic dishes: in Las Vegas you will find ethnic specialities from all over the world, with restaurants catering to many different tastes all at once. Wine connoisseurs also get their money's worth here. Many gourmet restaurants have excellent wine lists, which could compete with the best that France has to offer.

In addition, you will discover that in Las Vegas the meals are also a visual feast. Not only is the food beautifully garnished, but many places offer decoration changes in between the courses as well as stylish surroundings. Naturally, the restaurants expect that you dress accordingly, in elegant dress (shorts, jeans and gym shoes are not allowed). Foreigners not used to air-conditioning should take along some-

Endless delicacies – the Bellagio Hotel's buffet

thing warmer to put on! While it is almost 30° C/86° F degrees outside, inside you will find it a whole lot cooler.

Reservations are essential if you want to dine at the best restaurants (and even the mid category restaurants) because the demand for exclusive dining in attractive surroundings is massive. The *Mandalay Bay* offers the largest collection of top class restaurants, as do the *CityCenter* and the *Bellagio* – the newest trend is stylishly decorated lounge restaurants, which you will find in the Aria or at the Cosmopolitan – whilst you will find very good mid category restaurants in the *New York New York* and in *Caesars Palace*. Many also have affordable lunch menus which means that even the most gourmet of meals can actually be quite affordable.

Incidentally, the prices quoted always exclude tax (7.5 per cent) and service (15–20 per cent) And you should bear in mind that the tip is not just something extra for the waiter, but their only or main means of income. Also, do not get confused when reading the menu: with entrée (emphasis on the first syllable) they do not mean a starter, but rather the main dish. As always, Las Vegas is characterised by its many famous buffets. Despite some price hikes, you can still find a relatively wide selection of good quality, affordable food (average price between $10–25 and just 5–7 per cent tip for table and service, depending on the day of the week and the time of day). For those with a large appetite, you can even get the famous **INSIDER TIP** 'all you can eat' buffet which means you can come back to the buffet the whole day – and sometimes even in different hotels.

The majority of buffets do not accept reservations, so you will have to be patient and prepared to wait in long queues – especially at the top restaurants. You should either get there very early or really late, when the masses have left. Although Las Vegas is known as a city that never sleeps, most restaurants close before midnight (times indicated do not mean that the lights go out, rather the time for the last order). But this is not the case for all of them. Venues that are open 24 hours usually advertise graveyard specials, which they serve after midnight.

BUFFETS & BRUNCHES

BELLAGIO BUFFET ● (112 B4) (*ΩΩ B9*)
One of the most elegant buffets in Las Vegas, serving exquisite food in an elegant setting with a wide selection of different international cuisines. For instance, you can enjoy Italian, Japanese, Chinese or Mexican dishes. *Daily 7am–10pm (with short breaks for each new service) | $16–37 | in the Bellagio | 3600 Las Vegas Blvd S.*

CARNIVAL WORLD BUFFET
(112 A4) (*ΩΩ A8*)
Popular and multi award-winning. Here you have a large selection of tasty dishes from pizza to Asian barbecue and almost 70 different cakes and desserts. *Daily 8am–10pm | $16–25 | in the Rio | 3700 W. Flamingo Rd | bus 202 West from the corner Strip/Flamingo Rd*

HOUSE OF BLUES GOSPEL BRUNCH ★
(114 A2) (*ΩΩ B11*)
Food for both the body and the soul. Every Sunday a gospel choir from a different part of the country sings here, while the guests enjoy a real Southern buffet. *Sundays at different times | $37 | buy tickets in advance | in the Mandalay Bay | 3950 Las Vegas Blvd S. | tel. 702 6 32 76 00 | www.mandalaybay.com*

LE VILLAGE BUFFET
(112 C4–5) (*ΩΩ B–C9*)
Specialities from Burgundy and Alsace, from Provence and other French regions with delectable sauces for the various

meat dishes. Beautifully decorated venue, but very full (just as it would be in Paris). Sundays: bottomless Champagne. *Daily 7am–10pm | $16–28 | in the Paris | 3655 Las Vegas Blvd S. | tel. 702 9 46 70 00*

INSIDER TIP ▶ MAIN STREET STATION GARDEN COURT (111 E1) (*ΩΩ E1*)
Good quality, great selection. Different specialities depending on the day of the

---

week: Tuesday steaks, Thursday fillets and shrimps, Friday fish and seafood, including lobster. Very reasonable prices. *Daily 7am–10pm (with short breaks for each new service) | $7–18 | 200 N. Main St | Downtown | tel. 702 3 87 18 96 | bus 301*

MANDALAY BAY'S BAYSIDE BUFFET ⭐
(114 A2) *(𝄢 B11)*
Not very large but a great choice of excellent quality food in appealing surroundings. It manages an intimate atmosphere, despite the fact that it accommodates 500 guests. Large windows, with a view

of the extraordinary swimming pool (with a real beach). Try the delicious home-made desserts. *Daily 7am–2.30pm, 4.45pm–9.45pm | $14–26 | in the Mandalay Bay | 3950 Las Vegas Blvd S. | tel. 702 6 32 74 02*

RESTAURANTS: EXPENSIVE

AMERICAN FISH
(112 B5) *(𝄢 B9)*
Wooden floors and an artificial forest adds to the rustic style of the refined American seafood served by Michael Mina. Originally from Egypt, this star chef

GOURMET RESTAURANTS

Alizé ⭐ ⚔ (112 A4) *(𝄢 A8)*
Starve yourself a little beforehand so that you can enjoy all the food at Alizé. Excellent service, skilfully designed menu, huge wine selection and an attractive setting in a transparent cooling tower that has fantastic panoramic views of the city from the top. *Minimum $45, 5-course taste menu $105, 7-course taste menu $125 | daily from 5.30pm | 56th floor in the Palms | 4321 W. Flamingo Rd | tel. 702 9 51 70 00 | www.andrelv.com*

Aureole (114 A2) *(𝄢 B11)*
A combination of extremely elegant design, delicious creations by New Yorker, Charlie Palmer, and exquisite wines. Waitresses in black catsuits retrieve the wine from a glass enclosed wine tower. *3-course menu from $75 | Sun–Thu 6pm–10.30pm, Fri/Sat 5.30pm–10.30pm, lounge 6pm–midnight | in the Mandalay Bay | 3950 Las Vegas Blvd S. | tel. 702 6 32 74 01 | www.aureolelv.com*

L'Atelier de Joël Robuchon
(114 C6) *(𝄢 B–C10)*
Top class French dining, from the champion of gourmet chefs, in a relaxed and intimate atmosphere. Guests can sit at the bar and watch as the meals are created. They serve, amongst others, unusual combinations like hamburgers with foie gras and lobster with curry and fennel. *Menus from $75 | Sun–Thu 5.30pm–10.30pm, Fri/Sat 5pm–10.30pm | in the MGM Grand | tel. 702 8 91 73 58 | www.joel-robuchon.net*

Mix (114 A2) *(𝄢 B11)*
The French legend, Alain Ducasse built a dream kitchen (that cost 14 million dollars) high up in THEhotel at the Mandalay Bay Hotel complex. Here his team celebrates the finest of French cuisine – do go to the ⚔ Mix Lounge for drinks afterwards as the view is breathtaking. *Main dishes $30–50, tasting menus $90 | daily 6pm–11pm | in the Mandalay Bay | 3950 Las Vegas Blvd S. | tel. 702 6 32 95 00 | www.mandalaybay.com*

made a name for himself in San Francisco before he opened various restaurants in Las Vegas. Very good: trout from Idaho and black cod from Washington. *Tue–Sun 5pm–11.30pm | in the Aria | 3730 Las Vegas Blvd S. | tel. 702 5 90 86 10 | www. arialasvegas.com*

AQUAKNOX
(112 C3) (ⅅ C7–8)

Delicious fish dishes with ingredients that are flown in daily from all over the world. Stylish surroundings close to the Grand Canal. *Daily noon–3pm and Sun–Thu 5.30–10pm (bar noon–1am), Fri/Sat until 11pm (bar until 2am) | in the Venetian | 3355 Las Vegas Blvd S. | tel. 702 4 14 37 72 | www.venetian.com*

EIFFEL TOWER RESTAURANT ☆
(112 C3) (ⅅ B–C9)

A glass lift takes you straight into the 11th floor restaurant of the Eiffel Tower. Modern French cuisine and wonderful soufflés. The tables in the western part of the restaurant have a view of the Bellagio's water show. *Daily 11.30am–2.30pm, Mon–Thu also 5.30pm–10.30pm, Fri–Sun 5pm–11pm | in the Paris | 3655 Las Vegas Blvd S. | tel. 702 9 48 69 37 | www.eiffeltower restaurant.com*

INSIDER TIP ▶ FLEUR
(114 A2) (ⅅ B11)

Here they serve chic tapas and tasty snacks instead of expensive meals – and they also have an impressive selection of Californian wines. The cheerful young waiters present the unusual dishes by top chef Hubert Keller (who earned himself two Michelin stars in San Francisco) like little works of art. Very good wine list with many rare or unusual Californian wines. *Daily 11am–11pm | in the Mandalay Bay | 3950 Las Vegas Blvd S. | tel. 702 6 32 94 00 | www.mandalaybay.com*

Fleur – the creative cuisine of Hubert Keller started at Burger & Co.

INSIDER TIP ▶ LITTLE BUDDHA RESTAURANT (112 A4) (ⅅ A8)

A Parisian import. Fantastic interior, exotic atmosphere, successful Pacific and Chinese cuisine with French influences. Large sushi selection. *Daily from 5.30pm | in the Palms | 4321 W. Flamingo Rd | tel. 702 9 42 77 78 | www.littlebuddhalasvegas. com*

MICHAEL MINA
(112 B4) (ⅅ B9)

Elegant seafood restaurant with unconventional menu: have you ever tried seafood with foie gras, mussel soufflé or fish carpaccio? *Daily from 5.30pm | in the Bellagio | 3600 Las Vegas Blvd S. | tel. 702 6 93 72 23 | www.bellagio.com*

PICASSO (112 B4) (*Ⅲ B9*)

Fine southern French cuisine with a dash of Spanish flair. Elegant ambience with genuine Picasso paintings and sculptures as well as some wonderful flower arrangements. *Wed–Mon 6pm–9.30pm | in the Bellagio | 3600 Las Vegas Blvd S. | tel. 702 6 93 72 23 | www.bellagio.com*

INSIDER TIP ROSEMARY'S RESTAURANT (116 B3) (*Ⅲ O*)

Wendy and Michael have fulfilled their dream and now cook haute cuisine dishes from all the various regions of America. There is also a second *Rosemary's* in the *Rio Hotel*, somewhat less traditionally American and more expensive. Visit the original, even if it is a little out of the way. *Lunch only Fri 11.30am–2pm, dinner daily from 5.30pm | 8125 W. Sahara Ave | tel. 702 8 69 22 51 | www.rosemarysrestaurant. com | bus 204 West from Strip/Sahara Ave*

SW STEAKHOUSE ★ (112 C2–3) (*Ⅲ C7*)

Delicious, tender American steaks combined with Alsatian sauces and side dishes. The best is that from the ⌇ terrace you have a direct view of the *Lake of Dreams* and the nightly light show. *Daily 5.30pm–10pm | in the Wynn | 3131 Las Vegas Blvd S. | tel. 702 3 80 77 11 | www. wynnlasvegas.com*

TOP OF THE WORLD ⌇ (111 D5) (*Ⅲ D4*)

You do not only pay for the food, but also for the great view. The interior of the restaurant rotates, so you get a wonderfully panoramic view of the whole city from the 106th floor. The food is good, but not as exceptional as the prices. *Daily 11am–3pm and from 5.30pm, lounge from 4pm | in the Stratosphere | 2000 Las Vegas Blvd S. | tel. 702 3 80 77 77 | www.topofthe worldlv.com*

VOODOO STEAK & LOUNGE ★ ⌇ (112 A4) (*Ⅲ A8*)

Who knows what magic the chef uses to get his steaks this tasty. They specialise in a delicious fusion of American and Cajun Creole cuisine, guaranteed to be served without a curse. The dream view from the 50th floor will also have you spellbound! *Daily from 5pm | in the Rio | 3700 W. Flamingo Rd | tel. 702 7 77 79 23 | www. riolasvegas.com*

RESTAURANTS: MODERATE

BEIJING NOODLE NO. 9 ★ (112 B3) (*Ⅲ B8*)

An optical and culinary super-experience: the entrance is flanked by two huge aquariums and behind them is a venue that looks like an ice cave. Serving original Peking cuisine with classic noodle soups and fine dim sum dishes. The noodles are handmade at the counter and you should try the very tasty salt and pepper shrimps. *Sun–Thu 11am–11pm, Fri/Sat 11am–midnight | in Caesars Palace | 3570 Las Vegas Blvd S. | tel. 877 3 46 46 42 | www.caesars palace.com*

BOUCHON ★ ⊙ (112 C3) (*Ⅲ C7–8*)

Thomas Keller is regarded as one of the top five chefs in America and he has proven his status over the past couple of years with his two restaurants in California's Napa Valley. The Vegas venue is styled like a classic French oyster bar but the ingredients are American and are sourced from sustainable catches: the mussels are from Maine, the caviar from California. The small outside terrace is very romantic. *Mon–Fri 7am–10.30pm and daily 5pm–10pm, Sat/Sun brunch 8am–2pm, oyster bar daily 3pm–10pm | in the Venetian | 3355 Las Vegas Blvd S. | tel. 702 4 14 62 00 | www.venetian.com*

FOOD & DRINK

HOFBRÄUHAUS (113 E5) (*ψ D9*)

Want to try a German platter, some *spätzle* or a German sausage and beer? The Hofbräuhaus serves German specialities with American hospitality in an air-conditioned

MON AMI GABI
(112 C4–5) (*ψ B–C9*)

A comfortable bistro with good French cuisine at the foot of the Eiffel Tower. Mon Ami Gabi is one of the few restaurants

Mon Ami Gabi – a classic French bistro right on the busy Strip

beer hall decorated in the Bavarian blues and whites. *Sun–Thu 11am–11pm, Fri/Sat 11am–midnight | 4510 Paradise Rd | close to the Hard Rock Hotel | tel. 702 8 53 23 37 | www.hofbrauhauslasvegas.com*

HOUSE OF BLUES
(114 A2) (*ψ B11*)

Creole and Cajun specialities before the concert: seafood gumbo (fish soup), jambalaya (a casserole with various kinds of meat, sometimes also seafood) and *etouffée* (also a casserole dish with crawfish from Louisiana). *Sun–Thu 8am–midnight, Fri/Sat 8am–1am | in the Mandalay Bay | 3950 Las Vegas Blvd S. | tel. 702 6 32 76 07 | www.mandalaybay.com*

that has a ⚘ terrace directly on the Strip, along with a view of the Bellagio's water show. *Daily 9am–11pm, Sat until 2pm | in the Paris | 3655 Las Vegas Blvd S. | tel. 702 9 44 42 24 | www.monamigabi.com*

PLANET HOLLYWOOD
(112 B4) (*ψ B8*)

Famous movie restaurant with memorabilia and set props from the film world. American cuisine with Mexican and Italian influences: pizza, pasta, hamburgers, salads, steaks. *Sun–Thu 9am–11pm, Fri/Sat 9am–midnight | in Caesars Palace | 3500 Las Vegas Blvd S. | reservations only for 6 or more, often long queues | tel. 702 7 91 78 27 | www.planethollywoodintl.com*

Light Californian cuisine with European influences – Spago in Caesars Palace

RAINFOREST CAFÉ ★
(112 C6) (*ᗰ B–C10*)

Eat in a tropical jungle surrounded by vines and waterfalls, there are even 'animals' (like apes and elephants) in the rain forest making this the ideal venue for children. Not all the plants and animals are fake but the hungry crocodile is. American food with Mexican and Caribbean influences. *Daily 8am–11pm, Sat until midnight | in the MGM Grand | 3799 Las Vegas Blvd S. | tel. 702 8 91 85 80 | www.rainforestcafe.com*

SENSI ☺ (112 B4–5) (*ᗰ B9*)

International dishes prepared by chef Martin Heierling at the cooking station in the centre of the restaurant. The use of organic products and fish from sustainable catches are part of his cooking philosophy. *Mon–Thu 5pm–9.45pm, Fri–Sun 5pm–10.15pm | in the Bellagio | 3600 Las Vegas Blvd S. | tel. 1 866 2 59 71 11 | www.bellagio.com*

SPAGO (112 B4) (*ᗰ B8*)

The Austrian chef Wolfgang Puck started his training at the tender age of 14 in Provence and then took his knowledge to the American West Coast. Spago first opened in Los Angeles and later also in Las Vegas and is famous for its gourmet pizzas. They also serve great Californian Italian salads, pasta, fish and meat dishes. *Café and bar Sun–Thu 11.30am–11pm, Fri/Sat until midnight, restaurant daily 5.30pm–10pm | in Caesars Palace | 3570 Las Vegas Blvd S. | tel. 702 3 69 63 00 | www.wolfgangpuck.com*

YOLÖS MEXICAN GRILL
(112 C5) (*ᗰ B–C9*)

Mexican cantina with tasty steak dishes. Relaxed atmosphere. *Sun–Thu 11.30am–10pm (bar until midnight), Fri–Sat 11.30am–midnight (bar until 2am) | in Planet Hollywood | 3667 Las Vegas Blvd S. | tel. 702 7 85 01 22 | www.planethollywoodresort.com*

RESTAURANTS: BUDGET

BOUGAINVILLEA (113 E4) (*D8–9*)

American and Chinese cuisine that is both tasty and affordable, especially the roast meats from the rotisserie. Also *graveyard specials. Daily 24 hours (no reservations) | in the Terrible's | 4100 Paradise Rd | bus 202 East from corner of Strip/Flamingo Rd*

CAFÉ ÎLE ST. LOUIS
(112 C4–5) (*B–C9*)

Street café à la Parisienne. Breakfast around the clock with different European coffees (espresso, café au lait). French dishes afternoons and evenings. *Daily 24 hours (no reservations) | in the Paris | 3655 Las Vegas Blvd S.*

COURTYARD CAFÉ (0) (*0*)

American and spicy New Orleans cuisine at reasonable prices. A decent steak with different side dishes for only $18 – which is not something you will find often in Las Vegas. *Daily 24 hours | in the Orleans | 4500 W. Tropicana Ave | tel. 702 3 65 71 11 | bus 201 West from corner Strip/Tropicana Ave*

CYPRESS STREET MARKETPLACE
(112 B4) (*B8*)

Choose your own dishes from the different stalls and pay after eating. Salads, soups, pizzas, sandwiches, shrimps – American, Vietnamese, Chinese. You will find almost everything here, most for under $10. *Daily 11am–11pm (no reservations) | in Caesars Palace | 3570 Las Vegas Blvd S.*

DRAGON NOODLE (112 B6) (*B10*)

Every kind of Asian noodle dish made with fresh ingredients as well as traditional Chinese cuisine, often visited by Asian guests – which speaks volumes about the quality of the food. *Sun–Thu 10.30am–1pm, Fri/Sat 10.30am–midnight | in the*

Monte Carlo | 3770 Las Vegas Blvd S. | tel. 702 7 30 79 65 | www.montecarlo.com

INSIDER TIP DU PARIS GOLDEN GATE BAY CITY DINER (111 E1) (*E1*)

An American diner with prices, portions, design and service that harks back to the good ol' days. Delicious pancakes for breakfast! Have your starter at the *San Francisco Shrimp Bar* (in the same hotel). The shrimp cocktail with home-made cocktail sauce at only $1,99 is a still a winner. More than 40 million dishes have been sold since 1959! *Daily 24 hours | in the Golden Gate | 1 Fremont St | tel. 702 3 85 19 06*

LOW BUDGET

▶ Low prices away from the Strip: more and more of the large resorts that are not on the Strip itself try to make up for their location with low prices and this is where you will find some excellent buffets at very reasonable prices. West of the Strip, try the inexpensive prime rib in the *Cortez Room (Gold Coast Casino* **(112 A4)** (*0*)). While east of the Strip, *Mr. Lucky's* **(Hard Rock Hotel (113 E5)** (*D9*)) serves huge salads for $10. Close by is the *Bougainvillea Cafe* **(Terrible's (113 E4)** (*B8–9*)) serving for example, a Thai curry for $5,99.

▶ The food courts in the shopping malls are also a good source of cheap meals (e.g. in the *Fashion Show Mall* **(112 C2–3)** (*B7*)). You can get anything from pizza to Chinese sweet and sour and Mexican tortillas to ice-cream – and it is all self-serve.

LOCAL SPECIALITIES

▶ **BBQ honey glazed ribs** – ribs that have been marinated then slow cooked in the oven and finally barbecued on a hot grill

▶ **Blue corn pancakes with toasted pine nuts and honey butter** – a traditional Southern style pancake using Hopi maize

▶ **Butternut squash soup** – a delicious traditional American Indian squash soup

▶ **Chilli con carne (photo left)** – spicy stew with minced meat and chilli peppers flavoured with tomatoes, garlic and onions

▶ **Corn bread** – yellow maize bread, sweet or spicy

▶ **Crispy fried onion rings** – very popular snack in America, often served with burgers

▶ **Double chocolate fudge brownie (photo right)** – dark, sweet and calorie laden American classic

▶ **Ginger sweet potatoes** – often served as a side dish and also prepared with maple syrup or even marsh-mallows

▶ **Nachos** – corn chips baked with cheese and served with avocado and/or sour cream

▶ **Prime rib with horseradish** – prime rib is a classic American cut usually served pink with the horseradish giving it a spicy kick

▶ **Stuffed Portobello mushrooms** – usually with herbs or meat, baked or grilled

▶ **Sweet corn** – usually eaten on the cob and as an accompaniment to a barbecue

▶ **Tortilla chips** – chips that are made from maize flour thinly rolled out, cut into wedges and then fried, seasoned and served with guacamole and spicy salsa

HARD ROCK CAFE (112 C5) (*₥ B10*)
Simple, good and affordable. Burgers, sandwiches, steaks and more. You will immediately recognise the iconic guitar above the entrance. Admire Elvis' guitars, Madonna's jackets or Elton John's suits whilst dining. *Daily from 11am | 3771 Las Vegas Blvd S. | tel. 702 7 33 12 75 | www. hardrock.com*

HARLEY DAVIDSON CAFE (112 C5) (*₥ B9*)
A Harley-themed restaurant with motorcycles from Billy Joel, Elvis and other

Route 66 memorabilia. It has a huge replica bike bursting through the restaurant's front wall. Not only for rockers. American menu with Mexican Italian influences: sandwiches, meat and chilli dishes and pasta. *Sun–Thu 11am–midnight, Fri/Sat 11am–2am | 3725 Las Vegas Blvd S. | tel. 702 7 40 45 55 | www.harley-davidsoncafe.com*

KGB
(112 C3) ( B8)

The retro décor is a nod to the old Soviet Union, with Russian comic art on the walls. They serve very good hamburgers, tasty chips and other American dishes. KGB actually stands for Kerry's Gourmet Burgers. *Daily 11am–11pm | in the Harrah's | 3475 Las Vegas Blvd S. | tel. 702 3 69 50 65 | www.harrahslasvegas.com*

INSIDER TIP SERENDIPITY 3
(112 B4) (ω B8)

On the terrace in front of the Caesars Palace with a view of the Strip, you get to taste all kinds of sinfully delicious meals: honey-glazed ribs and moist Southern fried chicken, fabulous milkshakes and very sweet desserts. *Mon–Thu 11am–10pm, Fri 11am–midnight, Sat 10am–midnight, Sun 10am–10pm | in Caesars Palace | 3570 Las Vegas Blvd S. | tel. 702 731 73 73 | www.caesarspalace.com*

INSIDER TIP SONIC DRIVE IN
(112 A4) (ω O)

Burgers, milkshakes, soda and French fries – the classic all American fast food fare served in this popular chain of burger venues. The best bit is that they are just like the drive-ins from the 1950s, and you can watch a movie, order food and eat in your car. *Daily 6am–midnight | various venues in Las Vegas, for example: 4260 W. Flamingo Rd | tel. 702 8 73 43 28*

INSIDER TIP TIFFANY'S AT THE WHITE CROSS PHARMACY (111 D4) (ω D4)

The first restaurant in Las Vegas to be open around the clock, it has now been in business for over 60 years. Although the owners have changed over the years and the lunch counter has seen better days, not much else has changed. Sit at the bar and watch the chefs as they work. Grilled meat, hamburgers and highly popular milkshakes! *Daily 24 hours | 1700 S. Las Vegas Blvd | short walk north of the Stratosphere | tel. 702 4 44 44 59*

The iconic electric guitar outside the Hard Rock Cafe

SHOPPING

CITY **WHERE TO START?**
Las Vegas Premium Outlets North (110 C–D) (*D2*) and Las Vegas Premium Outlets South (116 B4) (*O*): A great alternative to the casino hotel boutiques, these two outlets – in the north and south – sell everything from clothing, shoes, sport accessories and leather goods at very reasonable prices.

Even a shopping spree can be an adventure in Las Vegas. All the large casinos have shopping galleries and some have hundreds of shops. Every gallery has its own character and they almost always offer some sort of free entertainment.

They are not always cheap as the casinos love to surround themselves with exclusive luxury shops so shopping arcades in the Bellagio and the MGM Grand are filled with expensive shops like Tiffany & Co., Cartier or Gucci, all just waiting for a new gambling millionaire or extravagant holidaymaker. The shops in malls like *Miracle Mile Shops* or *Fashion Show Mall* offer boutiques and department stores with more normal prices. Remember that all the prices are net, 8.1 per cent tax is only added on at the cashier.

Photo: Forum Shops at Caesars Palace

Cowboy hats and showgirl boas: original, cool, eccentric – get dressed for the Vegas nightlife

SOUVENIRS

CIRQUE DU SOLEIL LOVE BOUTIQUE
(112 B3) (𝄞 B7–8)
Beautiful souvenirs and merchandise from the famous show: dancer tee shirts, masks for children, jewellery, CDs and books. Each of the stage shows has a gift shop, for example for the show *Love* in the Mirage: *Thu–Mon 10am–12.30am,* *Tue/Wed 10am–8pm | 3400 Las Vegas Blvd S. | www.cirquedusoleil.com*

HARLEY DAVIDSON STORE
(O) (𝄞 H5)
Biker heaven: this is the largest Harley Davidson shop in the world. *Mon–Fri 8am–6pm, Sat 9am–6pm, Sun 10am–3pm | 2605 S. Eastern Ave | www.lasvegasharley davidson.com*

Fashion Show Mall – all your wishes will come true

CITTÀ DELLE LUCI (112 C3) *(ⓜ C7–8)*

Looking for tasteful Las Vegas souvenirs with an Italian touch? Here you will find tee shirts, hats, mugs, pens and other bric-a-brac with the Las Vegas logo. *Sun–Thu 10am–11pm, Fri/Sat 10am–midnight | in the Venetian | 3377 Las Vegas Blvd S.*

GALLERIES

INSIDER TIP ARTS FACTORY ☺
(111 D4) *(ⓜ D3)*

This gallery is the centre of the up-and-coming new *Arts District* in Las Vegas. Young or newly established artists and photographers can have exhibitions here or rent studios, where visitors are also wel-come. The building also houses a very creative bistro *(tel. 702 2 02 60 60)* and a shop. *Mon–Sat 9am–6pm | 107 E. Charleston Ave | www.theartsfactory.com | The Deuce up to Charleston, then bus 206 West*

CENTAUR ART GALLERIES
(112 C2–3) *(ⓜ B7)*

Pop-art, modern art, sculptures and prints. Also works by Salvador Dalí, Picasso, Rembrandt, James Whistler or Steve Kaufman, Andy Warhol's former assistant. *Mon–Sat 10am–9pm, Sun 11am–7pm | Fashion Show Mall | suite 1040, 3200 Las Vegas Blvd S. | www.centaurgalleries.com | The Deuce*

GAMBLING

GAMBLER'S BOOK CLUB
(116 C4) *(ⓜ H11)*

Here you will find books, videos and software that will give you everything that you ever wanted to know about gambling, from poker to horse racing or casino management. Information centre for professional gamblers, journalists and researchers – but most of their sales are over the Internet. *Mon–Fri 9am–5pm, Sat 10am–6pm | 5473 S. Eastern Ave | www.gamblers bookclub.com | bus 201 East from corner Strip/Tropicana, then bus 110 South to Eastern*

GAMBLER'S GENERAL STORE ★
(111 D3) *(ⓜ D2)*

Here you can either purchase some original Vegas souvenirs or buy items for your gambling evenings at home: dice, cards, chips and even roulette tables and equipment. Also books about gambling tricks, croupier peak caps and other fun memorabilia. *Daily 9am–6pm | 800 S. Main St | Downtown | www.gamblersgeneralstore. com | The Deuce up to Charleston Blvd, then bus 206 East*

CLOTHING

INSIDER TIP THE ATTIC
(111 D3) (*m D3*)

Flashy and funky, both in presentation and content with a large selection of vintage and second-hand clothing, some furniture and decorative objects. *Mon–Sat 10am–6pm | 1025 S. Main St | Downtown | www.atticvintage.com | The Deuce up to Charleston Blvd, then bus 206 West*

INSIDER TIP COWTOWN BOOTS
(113 F4) (*m F8*)

Incredible selection of high quality Western boots (for cowboys and cowgirls) on offer. Made from a variety of leathers like buffalo, ostrich, crocodile or snakeskin and in every style possible. Also hats, belts, jeans and shirts. *Mon–Sat 10am–7pm, Sun noon–6pm | 1080 E. Flamingo | www.cowtownboots.com | bus 202 East from corner Strip/Flamingo Rd*

SHEPLERS WESTERN WEAR (O) (*m O*)
Leather and long tassels, Western jackets and jeans, shirts, hats, belts and boots. *Mon–Sat 10am–8pm, Sun 11am–6pm | 4700 W. Sahara Ave | www.sheplers.com | bus 204 West from Strip/Sahara Ave*

CULINARY

INSIDER TIP WINE CELLAR & TASTING ROOM (112 A4) (*m A8*)

A treasure trove for wine lovers – some very rare and hard to find European and Californian wines – it is just like a wine museum with almost 50,000 bottles! Over 100 of the wines may be tasted (for a fee of course), and discover fun corkscrews and other wine souvenirs. *Mon and Thu 4pm–10pm, Fri/Sat 3pm–11pm, Sun 3pm–11pm | in the Rio Casino | 3700 W. Flamingo Rd | bus 202 West from corner Strip/Flamingo Rd*

MALLS/SHOPPING CENTRES

CRYSTALS AT CITYCENTER ★ ☺
(112 B5) (*m B9*)

A true 21st century luxury shopping mall in an energy efficient building that uses state of the art water recycling. Underneath the dramatic jagged roof – designed by architect Daniel Libeskind – you will find all the exclusive luxury brands side by side: Tiffany & Co., Louis Vuitton, Dior, Hermès and Miu Miu. *Daily 10am–midnight | in the CityCenter | 3720 Las Vegas Blvd S.*

FASHION SHOW MALL ●
(112 C2–3) (*m B7*)

Even by American standards this mall is gigantic. It has over two hundred shops, amongst them seven department stores. *Mon–Sat 10am–9pm, Sun 11am–7pm | 3200 S. Las Vegas Blvd | www.thefashionshow.com | The Deuce*

★ **Gambler's General Store**
Chips and cards – the perfect souvenirs → p. 64

★ **Crystals at CityCenter**
Elegant and eco-friendly – a cutting-edge mall → p. 65

★ **Forum Shops at Caesars**
Where the gods live → p. 66

★ **Wynn Esplanade**
Choice wares at choice prices → p. 66

★ **Las Vegas Premium Outlets North**
A wide selection at affordable prices → p. 67

MARCO POLO HIGHLIGHTS

Ripa de Monti – Venetian glass shop in the Grand

FORUM SHOPS AT CAESARS ★
(112 B4) (⌘ B8)

Eclectic range of shops all under blue Mediterranean skies, there are Roman fountains and statues as well as hourly shows. More than 150 shops varying from expensive to affordable, like Louis Vuitton, Christian Dior, Gucci and an Apple Store. *Sun–Thu 10am–11pm, Fri/Sat 10am–midnight | in Caesars Palace | 3570 Las Vegas Blvd S.*

GRAND CANAL SHOPPES
(112 C3) (⌘ C7–8)

Walk across St Mark's Square to the Grand Canal and take a gondola on the upper floor. A variety of shops, including some with typically Venetian products: *Il Prato* sells wonderful masks, costumes, marionettes, while *Ripa de Monti* sells glass and paper imported from Venice. *Sun–Thu 10am–11pm, Fri/Sat 10am–midnight | in the Venetian | 3377 Las Vegas Blvd S.*

MIRACLE MILE SHOPS
(112 B4) (⌘ B–C9)

The *Planet Hollywood* shopping mall attracts the funky, the young and the trendy. Reasonably priced clothing, jewellery and other accessories, small pieces of furniture and gifts are what you will find in its 170 shops. Browse through the *Betty Page Boutique* – where everything is 1950s style. Every hour a thunder storm erupts in front of Tommy Bahamas. *Sun–Thu 10am–11pm, Fri/Sat 10am–midnight | Planet Hollywood | Las Vegas Blvd S. | www.miraclemileshopslv.com*

SHOWCASE MALL (112 C6) (⌘ B–C10)

M&M's World is the largest attraction of this small mall. They sell the colourful chocolate sweets in its different original packaging and also offer tee shirts, magnets and ties, all with the M&M logo. If you have worked up a thirst from all the sweets, then visit *The World of Coca Cola*, a store that sells vintage bottles and other products with one of the world's most famous logo. *Shops open at different times | 3785 Las Vegas Blvd S. (next to the MGM Grand)*

WYNN ESPLANADE ★
(112 C2) (⌘ C7)

Exquisite and unique and also very, very expensive. Apparently you will only find the things that Steve Wynn himself likes. Shoes by Manolo Blahnik (Sex and the City) or a Ferrari Maserati showroom. *Sun–Thu 10am–11pm, Fri/Sat 10am–midnight | in the Wynn | 3131 Las Vegas Blvd S.*

MUSIC

ZIA RECORD EXCHANGE (0) *(🕮 H9)*
Large selection of new and used CDs, rock, punk, jazz and movie soundtracks. Local stars play here on Fridays and Saturdays. *Daily 10am–midnight | No. 17, 4225 S. Eastern Ave | www.ziarecords.com | bus 202 East corner Strip/Flamingo Rd*

OUTLET CENTERS

INSIDERTIP **FASHION OUTLETS OF LAS VEGAS** (116 B6) *(🕮 O)*
A good stop on your way to or from California: the shops are more or less the same but the majority are clothing shops. Sometimes the prices are even cheaper than in the outlets in Las Vegas. Additional attraction: Bonny and Clyde's bullet ridden car. *At the Interstate 15, Exit 1, in Primm about 31mi from Las Vegas*

LAS VEGAS PREMIUM OUTLETS NORTH ★ (110 C–D3) *(🕮 D2)*
From Polo Ralph Lauren to Nike, Gap, Levi's, Tommy Hillfiger and Timberland, all the famous American brands have shops at this discount mall. There are 150 shops altogether. If you are staying on the Strip then it is an idea to take a stroll here and combine it with a visit Downtown. *Daily 10am–9pm, Sun until 8pm | 875 S. Grand Central Parkway | www.premium outlets.com | Downtown Express, SDX or WAX Bus*

LAS VEGAS PREMIUM OUTLETS SOUTH (116 B4) *(🕮 O)*
There are 'only' 140 shops in this outlet at the southern end of the Strip. Also parking facilities for camper vans. *Daily 10am–9pm, Sun until 8pm | 7400 Las Vegas Blvd S. | www.premiumoutlets.com | The Deuce bus and other buses from the South Strip Transfer Terminal (SSTT).*

TATTOOS

STUDIO 21 TATTOO GALLERY (0) *(🕮 O)*
Well-established family business, light and friendly, with an art gallery. *Daily noon–9pm | 6020 W. Flamingo Rd | www.studio 21tattoo.com | Bus 202 West corner Strip/Flamingo Rd*

STARLIGHT TATTOO (114 A2) *(🕮 B11)*
The modern studio of the world famous tattoo artist Mario Barth, who has a number of celebrity stars as clients. He also does tattoos according to the Japanese and Samoan tradition. *Daily 10am–2am | in the Mandalay Bay | 3950 Las Vegas Blvd S. | www.starlighttattoolasvegas.com*

LOW BUDGET

▶ Original historic souvenirs need not be expensive. *Los Angeles Antiques* on the outskirts of Downtown offers a wonderful collection of memorabilia from old casinos: from gambling chips and neon signs to lovely decorative pieces. *Mon–Thu 10am–6pm, Fri/Sat until 8pm, Sun noon–5pm | 625 Las Vegas Blvd S. | lostvegas.vpweb.com | The Deuce bus)*

▶ Colourful accessories, new and second-hand wares – the selection at the *Fantastic Indoor Swap Meet* at the western edge of the city is huge. Many dealers, but the prices are good – and you can also negotiate. *Fri–Sun 10am–6pm | 1717 S. Decatur Blvd | www.fantasticindoorswapmeet.com | bus 204 West corner Strip/Charleston, then bus 103 South*

ENTERTAINMENT

CITY WHERE TO START?
When kicking off for the night you should first find yourself a good viewing point – like the **Marquee** in the **Cosmopolitan (112 B5)** (🗺 **B9**) – and then watch the sun set as the city's lights are turned on. Then simply take a wander through the-casinos in **Caesars Palace**, the **Venetian** or the **Paris**.

For people who love to stay up all night, Las Vegas is a paradise. You have to stay here for some time (and win a lot of money) to fully enjoy its amazing night life. And as it is in all big cities, Las Vegas is busiest on Friday and Saturday nights. All the big theme hotels lure visitors with acrobatics, magic or music shows, and in additional to those shows they often also have a comedy or cabaret show in a more intimate venue. An exceptional experience is to take in one of the performances of the Canadian *Cirque du Soleil*: they keep their audiences spellbound with a mixture of acrobatics, dance, music and theatre. Reservations are a necessity.

Vegas offers an bewildering variety of pubs and discos: clubs have drinks and dancing; bars have drinks, food, and music; lounges

Photo: Outdoor show in front of Treasure Island

From the cool of the Ice Bar to the heat of Caribbean rhythms: fantastic shows and unusual bars will keep you awake until dawn

have drinks and live music. Many restaurants are also clubs or are changed into one after dinner. If you have dinner you do not have to pay an entrance fee. The clubs have very strict dress codes, women usually pay less than men or if it is a ladies night they enter for free.

At *www.vegas.com* you can get so-called 'front of the line tickets' which means that you will automatically get a place at the front of the queue. An informative website with trends and reviews of nightclubs is *www.jackcolton.com*.

BARS, CLUBS & LOUNGES

INSIDER TIP ▶ THE BAR AT TIMES SQUARE (112 B6) (*🗺 B10*)

Two pianists go at it head to head on the Las Vegas Times Square and create the perfect atmosphere. Separate cigar rooms with a large variety. *Daily 11am–2.30am, programme from 8pm, then entrance $10 | in the New York New York | 3790 Las Vegas Blvd S.*

GHOSTBAR ☼ (112 A4) (*Ⓜ A8*)
Its shimmering blue and pink lighting makes everything look eerily cold rather than cool. However the view through three glass walls and from the terrace on the

Margaritaville – a seaplane as decoration in the country singer Jimmy Buffet's club

CLEOPATRA'S BARGE (112 B4) (*Ⓜ B8*)
Dance on an ornate replica of the Egyptian queen's barge. The boat itself floats and the dance floor actually gently rocks on the water. *Daily 8.30pm–3am, live music from 9.30 pm | in Caesars Palace | 3570 Las Vegas Blvd S.*

DRAI'S AFTER HOURS (112 C4) (*Ⓜ B9*)
As soon as the waiters have cleared the last tables, this French restaurant is turned into a party venue. Cool layout in red and black with palm trees, books and wide sofas. Deep house and trance music. *Thu–Sun 1am–dawn (dress code) | entrance $20 | in the cellar of Bill's Gamblin Hall and Saloon | 3595 Las Vegas Blvd S. | www.draislasvegas.com*

55th floor is unbeatable. Relatively small and very crowded, so it is best to arrive early. *Daily 8pm–4am (dress code) | entrance $20–30 | in the Palms | 4321 W. Flamingo Rd | www.palms.com*

HOGS & HEIFERS
(111 E1) (*Ⓜ E1*)
If you grow tired of all the chic and sophisticated Vegas venues and want something a little different then this at the right place. It is a rather rough saloon Downtown with a traditional country atmosphere, INSIDER TIP beautiful old Harleys at the entrance and almost every evening they have country and western or rock bands performing. *201 N. 3rd St | tel. 702 6 76 14 57 | The Deuce bus*

HOUSE OF BLUES LATE NIGHT ★
(114 A2) *(∅ B11)*

Every evening the concert hall transforms into a lively dance venue, mostly live music and rhythm and blues from all eras. If you prefer to be able to watch all the action from above then the best seats are in the ☆ gallery. *Entrance from $10 (dress code) | in the Mandalay Bay | 3950 Las Vegas Blvd S. | www.houseofblues.com*

MARGARITAVILLE ● (112 C4) *(∅ B–C8)*

The singer Jimmy Buffet believes that there is no better combination than that of good food and good music, so he opened a chain of restaurants and bars, one of them in Las Vegas. The centrepiece of the tropical themed venue is the three storey high *Volcano Bar*. Every volcanic eruption pumps a huge amount of Margarita into two massive blenders. If you are not on the dance floor then the ☆ **INSIDER TIP** balcony is the perfect place to relax with a drink in hand while you watch the passing life on the Strip below. *Sun–Thu 11pm–2am, Fri/Sat until 3am, live music 10pm–2am | in the Flamingo | 3555 Las Vegas Blvd S. | www.margaritavillelasvegas.com*

MARQUEE ★ ☆ (112 B5) *(∅ B9)*

This is a spin-off of the New York club and is also the meeting place for Las Vegas' beautiful people. LED light walls surround the dance floor, and from the massive *Boom Box* you can watch the lights of Las Vegas through huge glass windows. By day the fashionable and the wealthy lounge by the club's swimming pool. *Nightclub Mon, Sun–Fri 10pm–4am | in the Cosmopolitan | 3708 Las Vegas Blvd S. | www.marquee lasvegas.com*

MINUS 5 ICE BAR ● ☆
(114 A2) *(∅ B11)*

When the heat gets too much then cool off in this bar. It is decorated with ice sculptures, the temperature is kept at a constant minus 5 degrees and everything is made with ice, from the walls to the glasses. Jackets are provided! *Daily 11am–3am | in the shops at Mandalay Bay | 3950 Las Vegas Blvd S. | www.minus5experience.com*

★ **House of Blues Late Night**
A really popular venue, especially during weekends → p. 71

★ **Marquée**
Ultra cool club with a great view of the Strip → p. 71

★ **Rain**
Pyrotechnics and water shows all around the bamboo dance floor → p. 72

★ **Red Square**
Be transported to Russia: over one hundred types of vodka → p. 72

★ **Céline Dion, Elton John & Rod Stewart**
Experience world famous stars up-close → p. 75

★ **O**
Fantastic artistry in the water, on the ground and in the air → p. 77

★ **Viva Elvis**
Long live the king! Well, at least for two hours → p. 77

★ **Zumanity – Another Side of Cirque du Soleil**
Erotic show – provocative yet sophisticated → p. 77

MARCO POLO HIGHLIGHTS

Feel like some Russian caviar and vodka? Then you have to go to Red Square

MIX LOUNGE ● (114 A2) (B11)
Enjoy your cocktails up high with one of the best views of the city: even some of the toilets have panoramic windows! *Daily from 5pm (dress code) | entrance $20–25 | in THEhotel in the Mandalay Bay | 3950 Las Vegas Blvd S.*

NINE FINE IRISHMEN
(112 B6) (B10)
This authentic Irish pub was inspired by the story of nine Irishmen who all lived during the start of the 19th century and whose destiny was shaped in different ways by the Revolution of 1848. What about a dark beer followed by an Irish whiskey? Live music daily from 10pm. *Sun–Thu 11am–3am, Fri/Sat 11am–4am | in the New York New York | 3790 Las Vegas Blvd S. | www.ninefineirishmen.com*

THE PUB (112 B5) (B10)
Right at the back of the casino is where you will find one of the best brewery pubs on the Strip, with their own beer and 200 other beers from all over the world. All fresh from the tap! Weekends live music. *Sun–Thu until 11pm, Fri/Sat until 3am | in the Monte Carlo Casino | 3770 Las Vegas Blvd S.*

RAIN ★ (112 A4) (A8)
The entrance is through a futuristic tunnel of gold-coloured, mirror mosaics and it gives you a good idea of what awaits you inside: fantastic lighting effects, flashes, smoke and pyrotechnics. Computer generated water shows surround the bamboo dance floor. Usually house and techno music. *Fri/Sat from 11pm (dress code) | entrance $30 | in the Palms | 4321 W. Flamingo Rd | www.palms.com*

RED SQUARE ★
(114 A2) (B11)
Off beat décor with communist propaganda art, a headless statue of Lenin and a huge block of ice as the bar. This bar and restaurant has many Russian specialities on the menu, but it also takes into account the demise of the Cold War and offers American dishes. An impressive and extensive caviar selection and more than a hundred different types of vodka in the walk-in fridge. *Sun–Thu 4pm–1am, Fri/Sat 4pm–2am | reservations essential: tel. 702 6 32 74 07 | in the Mandalay Bay | 3950 Las Vegas Blvd S.*

SHADOW BAR
(112 B4) (*B8*)
Only in Las Vegas: sip on one of the many cocktails and watch the silhouettes of striptease dancers, who INSIDER TIP perform their well-choreographed routines behind transparent screens. *Sun–Thu 4pm–2am, Fri–Sun midnight–3am | in Caesars Palace | 3570 Las Vegas Blvd S.*

STUDIO 54 (112 C6) (*B–C10*)
The original club in New York set the disco trends during the 1970s. At the beginning of the evening they play disco and hip-hop music, later on it is techno and house music. There are go-go dancers on the dance floor and also in show cages above the dance floor. *Tue–Sat 10pm–dawn | entrance $10–20 | in the MGM Grand | 3799 Las Vegas Blvd S. | www.mgmgrand.com*

TAO NIGHTCLUB
(112 C3) (*C7–8*)
Asian decorated nightclub on a number of different levels. Spoiler alert: when you leave the club you will see models bathing in rose petals. Terrace with a view of the city. The music is hip-hop, house and rock. *Thu–Sat from 10pm, lounge 5pm–4am | entrance $20–30 | in the Venetian | 3355 Las Vegas Blvd S.*

INSIDER TIP **TOBY KEITH'S I LOVE THIS BAR & GRILL** (112 C3–4) (*B8*)
The country star himself is not in his club that often but you will get to see a country music band and a DJ perform every night. Also some very good up-and-coming talent. The restaurant serves Southern food. *Daily 11.30–2am, Fri/Sat until 3am, live music daily 9pm–2am | in Harrah's | 3475 Las Vegas Blvd S. | www.tobykeith.com*

BOOKS & FILMS

▶ **Leaving Las Vegas** – A romantic drama based on a memoir. The movie is about two people, whom life has not treated very well, meeting and falling in love in Las Vegas. With Nicolas Cage and Elizabeth Shue (1995)

▶ **Casino** – Riveting Mafia crime drama based on real-life events. Starring Robert de Niro and Sharon Stone and directed by Martin Scorsese (1995)

▶ **Ocean's Eleven** – Sophisticated robbery in the most well known of the luxury Las Vegas casinos. This crime caper stars George Clooney, Julia Roberts, Brad Pitt, Matt Damon and the Klitschko brothers (2001, sequels 2004 and 2007)

▶ **Hangover** – Comedy about a wild stag party in Las Vegas with many scenes that were shot in Caesars Palace (2009)

▶ **Inside Las Vegas** – A non-fiction account about the Mob, call girls, pimps and gamblers in Las Vegas who are all chasing the dream of the big win (2002). By Mario Puzo, the author of 'The Godfather'.

▶ **Poker Nation** – A memoir that almost reads like a novel. The author, Andy Bellin, gives an insight into what goes on behind the scenes in Las Vegas and a sneak peek into the soul of a professional poker player, his bluffs and tricks (2002)

It is not often that you will see the Tryst, one of the trendiest clubs in the city, this empty

TOD ENGLISH PUB (112 B5) (*⑭ B9*)
In comparison to the casinos, this pub is nice and quiet and you can have a good beer and some decent pub food (with truffle mayo). On the first floor of the shopping centre. *Daily until 1am | Crystals at CityCenter | 3720 Las Vegas Blvd S.*

TRYST (112 C2) (*⑭ C7*)
Located directly on the *Lake of Dreams* with a large waterfall. Partially outside, this club offers something that is becoming a trend in Las Vegas: fresh air! Sophisticated setting which is also reflected in the prices of the drinks. Hip-hop is the main music style. *Thu–Sat 10pm–4am | entrance $20–30 | in the Wynn | 3131 Las Vegas Blvd S. | www.trystlasvegas.com*

VANITY (113 E5) (*⑭ D9*)
Popular club, not least of all because of the music played, a mix of rock, house and hip-hop. You will not gain entrance according to your place in the queue – the doorman decides who gets to go in. *Fri–Sun 10.30pm–4am | entrance $20–40 | in the Hard Rock Hotel | 4455 Paradise Rd*

VOODOO LOUNGE ☆ (112 A4) (*⑭ A8*)
A fantastic view from the 51st floor and good drinks in an exotic atmosphere. Live music every night from 9pm (hip-hop and the Top 40). The best bit is the large terrace with panoramic view, on Fri and Sat there is an outside DJ. *Daily 5pm–3am | from 8pm | in the Rio | 3700 W. Flamingo Rd*

COMEDY CLUBS

Las Vegas is famous for its comedy clubs which not only host local stars and new up-and-coming comedians but also well known international celebrities like Jerry Seinfeld and Rita Rudner. Check the dates and line up for the *Improv Comedy Club (Harrah's),* the *Riviera Comedy Club (Riviera* and *Bugsy's Cabaret (Flamingo).* You can find the current programmes at *www.visit lasvegas.com.*

CINEMAS

CENTURY 18 ORLEANS (112 B6) (*⑭ O*)
Twelve cinemas with a wide selection of films. *Entrance $10 | in the Orleans | 4500 W. Tropicana Ave | tel. 702 2 27 34 56 | www.coastmovies.com | Bus 201 corner Strip/Tropicana Ave*

GALAXY NEONOPOLIS (111 E2) (*⑭ E9*)
Absolutely gigantic: 14 cinemas, some with digital sound and giant screens. *450 E. Fremont St | Downtown | entrance $9.50 | tel. 702 3 83 96 00 | www.galaxytheatres. com | bus 301*

NIGHT FLIGHTS

⚡ Experience the *City of Lights* by night. Take a helicopter flight over Las Vegas' sea of lights with *Maverick Helicopters (from $115 | tel. 702 2 61 00 07 | www.maverick helicopter.com).*

POOL PARTIES

Many hotels transform their INSIDER TIP swimming pools into nightclubs and discos under the stars. Some just serve cocktails, while others serve extensive buffets. The *Hard Rock Hotel*, the *Mandalay Bay* and the *Paris Las Vegas* even build massive stages for stars like Billy Idol, the Go-Gos or Susan Tedeschi. You will find the dates for the performances in the hotels like the *Venetian*, *Rio* and *Caesars Palace*.

NIKKI BEACH (112 B1) (*⑭ B–C10*)
A branch of the international chain of clubs with their trademark tropical pool party experience – parties are held day and night. Lots of young people and ac-

tion especially during the college spring break in March. You can even play blackjack in the swimming pool. *Daily from 11am | in the Tropicana | 3801 Las Vegas Blvd S. | www.nikkibeach.com*

SHOWS

CÉLINE DION, ELTON JOHN & ROD STEWART ⭐ (112 B4) (*⑭ B8*)
For an expensive but sensational evening: the three superstars have been performing their own shows here for the past couple

LOW BUDGET

▶ ● In the large hotels, up-and-coming bands and singers from all over the USA often perform over the weekends. Why not take in some music, for example in the *Indigo Lounge* in Bally's, the *Bond Bar* in the Cosmopolitan, the *La Scene Lounge* in the Venetian or the *Koi Lounge* in Planet Hollywood. You can relax and enjoy without worry about the cost as there are no cover charges. Sometimes it is not even necessary to order a drink.

▶ *Tix4Tonight* offers tickets to shows for the same day at half the normal price, as well as discounts on restaurant reservations *(tel. 1 800 2 69 84 99)* at places like the Hawaiian Marketplace *(3743 Las Vegas Blvd S.* **(112 B4)** *(⑭ B9))*, in front of the Fashion Show Mall *(3200 Las Vegas Blvd S.* **(112 C2)** *(⑭ B7))* and Downtown at the 4 Queens Hotel *(202 Fremont St* **(111 E2)** *(⑭ E9)).* *Daily 11am–8pm | tel. 1 877 8 49 48 68 | www.tix4tonight.com*

of years on the large concert stage, the Colosseum. *Tickets $55–250 | in Caesars Palace | 3570 Las Vegas Blvd S. | Tickets at 877 4 23 54 63 for Céline, tel. 888 4 35 86 65 for Elton John, tel. 800 7 45 30 00 for Rod Stewart | www.caesarspalace.com*

JUBILÉE! (112 C4) (*Ø B–C8*)

Classic Vegas topless revue. Over 70 show-girls in spectacular costumes with feather boas and gigantic head pieces, some weighing more the 33lbs. Almost all of them originals from the early days of the Jubilée. Three well known stories build the core of the show, *The sinking of the Titanic, Samson & Delilah, Ginger & Fred*. Dancers have to go down two flights of stairs to change their costumes. The INSIDER TIP *Backstage Walking Tour* gives you a view of life backstage *(Mon, Wed, Sat 11am | $15–18 | tel. 702/967 49 38)*. *Sat–Thu 7.30pm and 10.30pm | entrance from $60 | in the Bally's | 3200 Las Vegas Blvd S. | tickets tel. 1 80 02 37 74 69 | www.ballyslv.com*

LOVE (112 B3) (*Ø B7–8*)

Founded on the friendship between George Harrison (who passed away in 2001) and the founder of Cirque du Soleil, Guy Laliberté, 60 international artists bring the songs of the Beatles to life in a fantastic musical production. Before and after the show, the music continues with Beatles originals and remixes being played in the *Revolution Lounge (daily 6pm–4am)*. *Thu–Mon 7pm and 9.30pm | entrance from $70 | in the Mirage | 3400 Las Vegas Blvd S. | tickets tel. 1 800 9 63 96 34 | www.cirquedusoleil.com*

MYSTÈRE (112 C3) (*Ø B7*)

Cirque du Soleil's first Las Vegas show from 1993, which is said to have changed the city's entertainment industry forever. A colourful and energetic mixture of surreal circus and cabaret with breathtaking ac-robatics, comedy, amazing set and stage designs, costumes and music. *Sat–Wed*

The show 'Love' celebrates the musical heritage of the Beatles

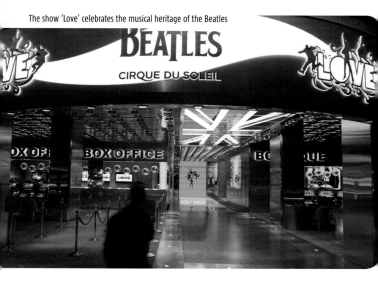

7pm and 9.30pm, Sun 4.30pm and 7pm | entrance from $60 | in the TI Treasure Island | 3300 Las Vegas Blvd S. | tickets tel. 702 8 94 77 22 | www.treasureisland.com

O
(112 B4) (∭ B9)

'O' as in the French eau – water the tonic of life. The water show of the *Cirque du Soleil* is all about the themes of life, love and death. Performers dive from 164ft into a 1.5 million gallon swimming pool and only surface again after a few minutes. Not visible to the audience, they follow the show from underwater, breathing oxygen fed through regulators. Incredibly perfect synchronised swimmers with costumes made from special material that looks like it is moulded to the swimmer's body. *Wed–Sun 7.30pm and 10.30pm | entrance from $95 | in the Bellagio | 3600 Las Vegas Blvd S. | tickets tel. 702 6 93 77 22 | www.bellagio.com*

VIVA ELVIS!
(112 B5) (∭ B9)

While the King himself may not perform in this high-energy Cirque du Soleil show, he is surely there in spirit as his songs are perfectly interpreted. This homage to Elvis includes great dancers and backdrops with a wonderful retro flair. A must see for all rock 'n roll fans. *Tue–Sat 7pm and 10.30pm | entrance $69–175 | in the Aria | 3730 Las Vegas Blvd S. | tickets tel. 702 5 90 77 60 | www.arialasvegas.com/viva-elvis*

ZUMANITY – ANOTHER SIDE OF CIRQUE DU SOLEIL
(112 B6) (∭ B10)

When *Cirque du Soleil* decided to create an erotic show they ended up producing something very unusual. 'Zumanity' is a word play on the words zoo and humanity and plays on the animal lust lurking inside humans. With performers and art- ists from all backgrounds and in all shapes and sizes. The show is artistically sophis- ticated, provocative (uninhibited) and ex- citing. Absolutely great! *Wed–Sun 7.30pm*

'O' – the Cirque du Soleil's spec- tacular water show in the Bellagio

and 10.30pm | entrance from $69 | in the New York New York | 3790 Las Vegas Blvd S. | tickets tel. 702 7 40 68 15 | www. zumanity.com

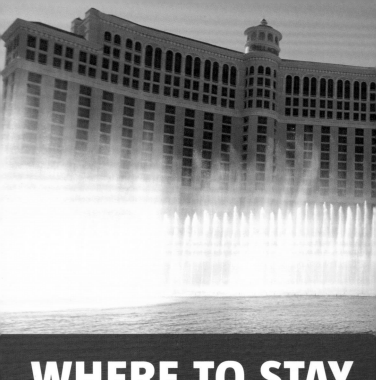

WHERE TO STAY

A hotel with less than 1000 rooms is regarded as 'cosy' in Las Vegas. The larger themed hotels are closer to the 4000 room mark some even exceed that number. Every year sees new construction and there are new towers constantly springing up, turning the giants into mega-giants. The latest property crisis seems to have had only a marginal impact.

The latest trend is to give the towers their own name and own character. Some market the fact that they have balconies, others bank on being casino free. The new hotels are almost exclusively luxurious and expensive. While the recession has put the brakes on the city's building boom but it

has not stopped it completely and there new complexes going up all the time so it is a good idea, when making your reservations, to ask if there are any building works around the hotel. Also consider this: the larger the hotel, the further you have to walk to reach your room.

Most hotels are designed so that guests arrive in the casino area which doubles as the foyer. Guests are drawn straight to the slots or gambling tables and this is exactly what is so appealing about a visit here, this city really makes it easy for visitors to experience everything.

Almost all the main attractions and sights are concentrated on the Strip and Down-

Photo: Fountains at the Bellagio

There is very little time to sleep in Las Vegas but when you do, you will find some rather novel accommodation and reasonable prices

town which often means that the traffic is very congested and you could miss the start of your show. This is something to bear in mind when you decide where you want to stay. If you do not like long walks, long drives or waiting then you should stay as centrally as possible or consider the monorail connections.

The best option is to stay directly on the Strip – right in the middle of all the glam-our and the neon lights – it is worth it. The smaller hotels away from the Strip are really only cheaper over weekends. And while you can enjoy the attractions of all the casino hotels without having to stay there, the lavishly designed swimming pools and landscapes are restricted to hotel guests.

You can choose between queen-size or king-size beds in most of the hotels. You

Magnificent view of the Loews Lake Las Vegas

front of the panoramic windows open automatically. The hotel has also installed cutting edge water recycling and sustainable technology and is exceptionally green by American standards. With swimming pool, spa and stylish restaurants. *4000 rooms | 3730 Las Vegas Blvd S. | tel. 702 5 90 77 57 | www.arialasvegas.com*

CAESARS PALACE (112 B4) (*M B8*)
One of the oldest (1966) and most characteristic of the Las Vegas hotels. The older deluxe rooms – as the simplest rooms are called – sometimes appear somewhat worn, but the higher categories are well furnished, many with marble baths, whirlpools and mirrored ceilings. The *Garden of the Gods* is a fantastic set-up with three swimming pools and a spa. *2500 rooms | 3570 S. Las Vegas Blvd | tel. 702 7 31 71 10 | www.caesarpalace.com*

HARD ROCK HOTEL ★ (113 E5) (*M D9*)
Today's hip music scene and the rock fans of the 1960s unite in their love for music at this rock temple. The décor includes a massive neon guitar, rock memorabilia and their own concert stage. Spacious rooms in a very retro style, attractive swimming pool area and beautiful spa facilities. *1700 rooms | 4455 Paradise Rd/corner Harmon Ave | tel. 702 6 93 50 00 | www.hardrockhotel.com | hotel shuttle to the Strip (Caesars Palace)*

LOEWS LAKE LAS VEGAS ●
(116 C4) (*M O*)
For golfers and everyone wishing to escape the casino hurly-burly. An elegant resort hotel with a Moroccan feel, with beautiful swimming pools, a sandy beach on Lake Las Vegas and surrounded by golf courses. Often very reasonable during midsummer. *490 rooms | 101 Montelago Blvd | Henderson | tel. 702 5 67 60 00 | www.loewshotels.com*

won't find any ordinary single beds and you should also state whether you would prefer a smoker or non-smoker room. And remember this: the higher your room, the better your view!

Lots of the cheaper motels, where you can park your car right in front of your room door, offer a simple continental breakfast of croissants or muffins and coffee or tea. Almost all the large hotels provide this option along with free parking for guests and visitors.

HOTELS: EXPENSIVE

ARIA ★ ☺ (112 B5) (*M B9*)
This extensive casino hotel is the heartbeat of the new CityCentre complex and offers ultra modern rooms with dark wood overtones. A very nice touch is that on entering your room, the curtains in

MGM GRAND (112 C6) (*Ø B–C10*)
One of the largest hotels in the world. The *Grand Tower* has spacious rooms that are tastefully decorated in a 1930s style. Beautiful black and white photographs from the glamour world of film stars. In the *Emerald Tower* the accommodation is cheaper and more modest. Large swimming pool area and spa. *6850 rooms | 3799 S. Las Vegas Blvd | tel. 702 8 91 77 77 | www.mgmgrand.com*

MIRAGE (112 B3) (*Ø B7–8*)
The first modern themed luxury hotel and the one with which mogul Steve Wynn ushered in a whole new era in 1989. By now it belongs to the older generation of theme hotels but it has retained its good reputation with some costly renovations. To get to the hotel rooms you go through a tropical rain forest, past orchids and waterfalls. The rooms themselves are decorated in a classically elegant style. They are not as spacious as some of the other hotels, but comfortable. Fine spa and two swimming pools surrounded by palm trees. *3000 rooms | 3400 S. Las Vegas Blvd | tel. 702 7 91 71 11 | www.mirage.com*

PARIS LAS VEGAS ❄
(112 C5) (*Ø B–C9*)
A miniature Paris with rooms overlooking the Eiffel Tower and the Bellagio's water ballet. The rooms might not have been good enough for the Sun King but they are tasteful and very elegantly decorated. Attractive bathrooms with deep baths. Beautiful spa and a swimming pool at the foot of the Eiffel Tower. *2900 rooms | 3655 S. Las Vegas Blvd | tel. 702 9 46 70 00 | www.parislasvegas.com*

THE RIO (112 A4) (*Ø A8*)
It is carnival all year here. The Rio only has suites, all of which come with living areas, walk-in dressing rooms and fridges. Attractive swimming pool area with waterfalls and a sandy beach. A very nice hotel that is unfortunately a bit remote, but they do have a shuttle to the Strip *(Harrah's Hotel)* every 30 minutes. *2580 rooms | 3700 W. Flamingo Rd | tel. 1 86 67 46 76 71 | www.riolasvegas.com | bus 202 West from corner Strip/Flamingo Rd*

⭐ **Aria**
Ecologically cutting edge – modern living in the new CityCentre → p. 80

⭐ **Hard Rock Hotel**
Live like a celebrity and mingle with rock legends → p. 80

⭐ **The Venetian**
Lavish luxury at the Grand Canal → p. 82

⭐ **Bellagio**
Aristocratic elegance and luxury – right on the lake → p. 82

⭐ **Cosmopolitan**
Trendy hot spot with rooms by star designer David Rockwell and great views → p. 82

⭐ **Mandalay Bay**
Colonial elegance – a pool landscape with lush palm trees, a white sandy beach and waves → p. 84

⭐ **Main Street Station**
Decorated with antiques from all over the world → p. 86

⭐ **Orleans**
The charm of the Deep South → p. 87

MARCO POLO HIGHLIGHTS

HOTELS: EXPENSIVE

SIGNATURE (112 C6) *(🕮 B–C10)*
The three new luxury towers of the *MGM Grand* only consist of suites, many with balconies. Excellent service and elegant furnishings. *Three towers each with 576 rooms | 145 E. Harmon Ave, close to the Strip | tel. 187 76 12 21 21 | www.signature mgmgrand.com*

THE VENETIAN ⭐ (112 C3) *(🕮 C7–8)*
The rooms on St Mark's Square and the Grand Canal are definitely not basic. They only have suites and they are all lavish. Comfortable living areas with sleeper couches, canopies over the beds and marble bathrooms. Their ultra luxurious suites are in the new *Venezia Tower*. Excep-

LUXURY HOTELS

Bellagio ⭐ (112 B4) *(🕮 B9)*
One of the most prestigious hotels on the Strip with extremely plush, elegant rooms, spacious bathrooms and excellent service. ⚜ The rooms that face the Strip also have a view of the water ballet. Six swimming pools in a beautifully landscaped Roman garden and a very luxurious spa and fitness centre. *From $169 | 3900 rooms | 3600 S. Las Vegas Blvd | tel. 702 6 93 71 44 11 | www.bellagio.com*

Cosmopolitan ⭐ (112 B5) *(🕮 B9)*
New and ultra chic: with video art in the foyer and a giant Swarovski chandelier three floors high. The contemporary suites and spacious rooms have been styled with dark wood by star designer David Rockwell. Many of the rooms have balconies, on the northern ⚜ side some even have a view of the Bellagio's water show. Very good restaurants and from the elegant pool deck (with three swimming pools) you can look out over the Vegas Strip. *From $170 | 3000 rooms | 3708 Las Vegas Blvd S. | tel. 702 6 98 70 00 | www.cosmopolitanlasvegas.com*

Four Seasons ⚜ (110 A2) *(🕮 B11)*
Famous for its unrivalled reputation for excellent service, the Four Seasons occupies the upper five floors of the Mandalay Bay and offers – in stark contrast to the noisy casino life all around – a wonderfully peaceful oasis. Extremely elegant fittings and furnishings. The use of the facilities of the Mandalay Bay are also included. *From $179 | 400 rooms | 3950 S. Las Vegas Blvd | tel. 702 6 32 50 00 | www.fourseasons.com*

THEhotel (114 A2) *(🕮 B11)*
The luxury tower, which also belongs to the Mandalay Bay, is styled entirely with black and cream tones. Asian influenced, clean architecture and only the best fittings. No casino. *From $120 | 1100 suites | 3950 S. Las Vegas Blvd | tel. 702 6 32 77 77 | www.mandalaybay. com/thehotel*

Wynn Las Vegas (112 C2–3) *(🕮 C7)*
Modern and elegantly furnished rooms and suites, with ⚜ a fantastic view of the picture-perfect golfing greens at the back. The hotel has a great ambience and an elegantly subdued atmosphere, the rooms all have spacious and tasteful bathrooms. The swimming pool is set in a lush landscape and there is also a rather impressive spa. *From $199 | 2700 rooms | 3131 S. Las Vegas Blvd | tel. 18773 21 99 66 | www.wynn lasvegas.com*

Video art in the reception area of the luxury Cosmopolitan

tional spa, a fitness centre with climbing wall and three swimming pools. *4000 rooms | 3355 S. Las Vegas Blvd | tel. 702 4 14 10 00 | www.venetian.com*

HOTELS: MODERATE

ALEXIS PARK (113 D5–6) (𝄢 D9)
Lovely, quiet hotel with two-storey bungalow-like buildings set in landscaped gardens with palm trees and fountains. No casino, no high-rises just classically elegant suites each with their own private access to the gardens. Three swimming pools and lots of greenery. *500 rooms | 375 E. Harmon Ave, two blocks from the Strip | tel. 702 7 96 33 00 | www.alexispark.com*

BALLY'S (112 C4) (𝄢 B–C8)
This hotel does not have a lake or a roller coaster, it is not a theme hotel and its casino looks a bit old but despite this its location – right in middle of the Strip next to the *Paris* – is absolutely perfect. All the rooms are spacious, newly renovated and well furnished. *2800 rooms | 3645 S. Las Vegas Blvd | tel. 702 7 39 41 11 | www.ballys lasvegas.com*

FLAMINGO LAS VEGAS
(112 C4) (𝄢 B–C8)
The oldest hotel on the Strip may be good for a trip down memory lane but since its opening 1946 by the Mobster Bugsy Siegel, a lot has changed. The paint may be peeling but it does offer large, decently furnished rooms in a very central location. Five swimming pools as well as water slides, all in a Caribbean landscape with streams, fountains and lagoons. *3600 rooms | 3555 S. Las Vegas Blvd | tel. 1 888 9 02 99 29 | www.flamingolasvegas.com*

DESERT ROSE RESORT
(114 B1) (*∅ C10*)

Spacious suites in an apartment complex with balconies and fully equipped kitchens, one block away from the Strip. The room rate includes breakfast – unusual for Las Vegas – and it is not just a continental breakfast, but also a proper breakfast buffet and even a happy hour with snacks in the afternoon. Swimming pool and a small fitness centre. *280 rooms | 5051 Duke Ellington Way | tel. 702 7 39 70 00 | www. desertroseresort.com*

HILTON LAS VEGAS (113 D1) (*∅ D6*)

This is not exactly the prettiest of hotels and it is also away from the Strip. But it is ideally located for conference goers – and when there is no conference on the go the room rates are really reasonable. It also has a swimming pool and spa. *3170 rooms | 3000 S. Paradise Rd | tel. 702 7 32 51 11 | www.hilton.com*

LOW BUDGET

▶ Accommodation in Las Vegas is noticeably more expensive on Friday and Saturday nights, so if you are given the choice then try to time your arrival for a Sunday.

▶ The *USA Hostel Las Vegas* **(111 F2)** (*∅ E1*) is a very comfortable youth hostel with Jacuzzi, swimming pool, billiards, ping-pong tables, Internet access and a well equipped kitchen. A daily pancake breakfast and a Sunday barbecue are included in the price, as is the cost of your transport to the bus or train station. *1322 Fremont St | Downtown | tel. 702 3 85 11 50 | www.lasvegashostel.net*

LUXOR (114 A2) (*∅ B11*)

Why not live like a pharaoh? At this hotel even the ride in the lift (angled at 39 degrees) up to the 30th floor of the pyramid is an experience. Be sure to ask for a renovated room as the old rooms really need some attention. Generous swimming pool area and a spa. *4400 rooms | 3900 S. Las Vegas Blvd | tel. 702 2 62 44 44 | www. luxor.com*

MANDALAY BAY ★
(114 A2) (*∅ B11*)

Colonial atmosphere with a tropical Pacific island theme. Spacious and decently furnished rooms with lovely bathrooms. The layout is well thought out with a casino that is separate from the hotel. It is connected to the Luxor and to the Excalibur by its own elevated railway. Great spa facilities, massive fitness centre and no less than ● six swimming pools, one of which has waves and a real beach! *3300 rooms | 3950 S. Las Vegas Blvd | tel. 702 6 32 77 77 | www.mandalaybay.com*

NEW YORK NEW YORK
(112 B6) (*∅ B10*)

The rooms (in 64 different styles) are divided into different towers, all of them with New York names and decorated in the art deco style. Oddly enough the larger and more expensive rooms are not as stylish as the more modest ones. Some of which are just as small as those you find in New York. INSIDER TIP Avoid the rooms that are close to the roller coaster because of the noise! *2000 rooms | 3790 S. Las Vegas Blvd | tel. 1 86 68 15 43 65 | www.newyork newyork.com*

PLANET HOLLYWOOD
(112 C5) (*∅ B–C9*)

This was once the oriental themed *Aladdin Hotel* and it has risen from the ashes to become a trendy favourite amongst the

The Luxor pyramid, guarded by its ten-storey tall sphinx

stars and starlets from Hollywood. Not surprising, as this is also the venue for the annual Miss America pageant. Stylish and modern rooms and some large shopping arcades. *2400 rooms | 3667 Las Vegas Blvd S. | tel. 702 7 85 55 55 | www.planethollywoodresort.com*

TI TREASURE ISLAND (112 C3) (*M C7*)

The smaller more affordable little sister to the Mirage is trying to find its own image. Here and there you will still see some remnants from the pirate era of *Treasure Island* in the foyer and rooms, but the overall style is that of French colonialism. Attractive bathrooms and enough space and comfort. A swimming pool surrounded by palm trees, a nice spa and the Sirens show right on your doorstep. *2900 rooms | 3300 S. Las Vegas Blvd | tel. 702 8 94 71 11 | www.treasureisland.com*

HOTELS: BUDGET

AMERICA'S BEST VALUE INN
(114 B1) (*M C10*)

A motel sans casino with clean and comfortable rooms that are simple and fuss-free. Only a block away from the excitement of the Strip. It also has its own attractive swimming pool. *250 rooms | 167 E. Tropicana Ave | tel. 1 817 3 33 52 12 | www.americasbestvalueinn.com | bus 201 East from corner Strip/Tropicana Ave*

BEST WESTERN MARDI GRAS INN
(113 D3) (*M D7*)

Motel with spacious suites in different sizes, all with living rooms and kitchens, free shuttle to the Strip. *300 rooms | 3500 Paradise Rd | tel. 702 7 31 20 20 | www.mardigrasinn.com | bus 203 from the corner Strip/Sands Ave or Monorail*

Even the inexpensive Motel 6 has its own swimming pool

EXCALIBUR (114 A1) (*ω B10*)
Medieval castle with turrets and a draw-bridge. One of the largest amongst the themed hotels but also one of the cheapest, with correspondingly basic furnishings. A lot of hustle and bustle. Be aware that the *New York New York* roller coaster can be disturbing if you are in *Tower 2*. *4000 rooms | 3850 Las Vegas Blvd S. | tel. 702 5 97 77 77 | www.excalibur.com*

GOLDEN GATE (111 E1) (*ω E1*)
Opened in 1906, this is one of the oldest hotels in the city. It has kept its originality and charm and is regarded as INSIDER TIP the most historic casino in the city. The prices have of course moved with the times, but not as much as other places and the rooms are all very nicely furnished. No swimming pool. *106 rooms | 1 Fremont St | Downtown | tel. 1 800 4 26 19 06 | www. goldengatecasino.com | bus SDX*

GOLDEN NUGGET (111 E2) (*ω E1*)
A well appointed hotel with some old-fashioned glamour and charm. It is one of Downtown's best hotels and has recently been renovated. The swimming pool is

exceptional because it allows you to swim with sharks (separated by glass of course) *2300 rooms | 129 E. Fremont St | Downtown | tel. 702 3 85 71 11 | www.golden nugget.com | bus SDX*

MAIN STREET STATION ⭐
(111 E1) (*ω E1*)
A hotel that has been decorated with attention to historical detail. Simple but elegantly furnished rooms. Even though the hotel is well insulated it is best to ask for a south facing room so that you can avoid the train noise on the north side. The neighbouring hotel's roof terrace swimming pool is available for use at no additional cost. *400 rooms | 200 N. Main St | Downtown | tel. 702 3 87 18 96 | www. mainstreetcasino.com | bus SDX*

MOTEL 6 (114 B1) (*ω C10*)
One of the cheapest motels in the city but the accommodation is quite acceptable, with a swimming pool and in a good location not far from the MGM Grand. *600 rooms | 195 E. Tropicana Ave | tel. 702 7 98 07 28 | www.motel6.com | Bus 201 East from the corner Strip/Tropicana Ave*

ORLEANS ⭐
(112 B6) (🏛 O)

A Disney version of New Orleans but done in a charming old French style. Opulently decorated, L-shaped rooms with cosy lounge corners at the windows. Also two swimming pools, a fitness centre and a spa. Regular shuttle to the Strip *(Barbary Coast)*. *1900 rooms | 4500 W. Tropicana Ave | tel. 702 3 65 71 11 | www.orleans casino.com | bus 201 West from corner Strip/Tropicana Ave*

INSIDER TIP TROPICANA RESORT
(112 C6) (🏛 B10)

In the best location directly next to the MGM, one of the older hotels on the Strip and also the location for movies like James Bond 'Diamonds are Forever'. Good value for money as most of the rooms have been newly renovated, the outsized swimming pool also has a new tropical design. *1800 rooms | 3801 Las Vegas Blvd S. | tel. 702 7 39 22 22 | www.troplv.com*

INSIDER TIP TERRIBLE'S
(113 E4) (🏛 D8–9)

It definitely does not live up to its name, on the contrary. Given the really low prices this casino hotel is actually really attractive. Obviously the rooms are very basic, but they are also neat and welcoming. They vary dramatically in size, so you have to ask for a spacious room. The swimming pool is surrounded by lush gardens. The hotel gets its name from the owner, Ed 'Terrible' Herbst. *370 rooms | 4100 Paradise Rd corner Flamingo | tel. 18173 33 52 12 | www.terriblescasono.com | bus 202 East from corner Strip/Flamingo Rd*

CAMPING

CIRCUS CIRCUS KOA
(110 C6) (🏛 C5)

Large campsite for camper vans with 400 spaces. Centrally situated right behind the CircusCircus Casino at the northern end of the Strip. *500 Circus Circus Dr | tel. 800 5 62 72 70 | www.circuscircuskoa.com*

SAM'S TOWN RV PARK
(116 C4) (🏛 O)

Cheaper, larger campsite next to Sam's Casino at the eastern outskirts of Las Vegas. Landscaped with a number of swimming pools and a laundrette. *5111 Boulder Hwy | tel. 702 4 56 77 77*

THE PRICE IS RIGHT

Nowhere else in the world does supply and demand influence hotel prices as extremely as in Las Vegas. Just like the airlines: every day, every flight has a new price, designed to maximise profit and to attract guests on the down days. So when business is slow in the middle of the week, say on a Tuesday, a room in an exclusive hotel can cost as little as 59 dollars and then next day when a trade fair starts and the city is full, the same room will cost you $249.

On the websites, prices are shown months in advance but a visit to a travel agency is also worthwhile: sometimes travel agents have a set rate for rooms which can even be cheaper during trade fairs or over the holiday season making them a better option than booking online. And the 12% hotel tax is included when making reservations through a travel agent.

LAS VEGAS SPECIAL

GAMBLING

● **In Las Vegas you are able to start gambling even before you have really arrived in the city: there are slot machines waiting for you at the airport.**

90 per cent of the city's tourists spend at least few hours every day at the card tables or on the casino floor at the slot machines, spending an average of about $500. Some of them are able to have a great time gambling a mere $20–30, while there are others who are happy to spend four, five, or six figure amounts – these are known as the high rollers. High rollers get special

treatment for their custom: limousine drives, restaurant meals, discounts on their accommodation or sometimes even free accommodation.

Even as a casual gambler it is certainly worth your while to get a *players club card* in one (or more) of the casinos of your choice. You insert it into the slot machine every time you play, or hand it to the dealer at the table, and depending on the length of play and the amount of money you spend, you will be given points which you can then exchange for vouchers which in turn give you discounts on hotel rooms or show tickets. You can also use them in the hotel gift shops or restaurants. If you

Lucky at cards and lucky in love – in Vegas you can have both – and you can find your hole-in-one on the city's manicured greens

have enough patience, you might also get a free drink (a soft drink or a cocktail) from one of the passing waiters whilst you are playing.

Both gambling and entry to the casinos is only for those over 21 so it is important to carry your proof of identity with you at all times. Should you be so lucky to win a large sum of money you will also be required provide proof of identity.

On the casino floor the dealers do not play with cash, only with chips. Chips are obtained from the cashier or directly at the table. You may also use cash at some of the tables (like the roulette table) but you will only receive chips back from the dealer, which you then exchange for cash when you leave the casino. Slot machines and other playing machines operate with cash and notes but most winnings are

Roulette – each player has a chip colour

paid out as bar coded tickets, which you can then either re-use at the slot machines or cash in at the casino box office cashier.

If you have never gambled before this is not a hindrance in Las Vegas. If there is not a lot happening, the casino dealers will happily answer all your questions. Many casinos also offer INSIDER TIP *free gaming lessons* during the week, these complimentary sessions teach the most important aspects of the game. Anyone can take part and you usually need not make a reservation. Make enquiries and arrive on time so that you get a spot at a table and secure the opportunity to take part in a test game.

The teachers are extremely friendly and patient. After all, they are there to encourage a love for the game. They teach the basic rules, the strategy and the etiquette as well as giving you hints, a few tricks and the jargon – all of which will increase your chances of winning. The casinos won't have a problem with this, because the odds are stacked in their favour and their chances of winning are always greater.

Before you join a game first observe the other players, listen to their words and watch their gestures. Some of the games, like blackjack and poker, can also be played on the monitors that can be found on many of the bar counters. Sometimes if you bet a certain amount of money (usually $10) you get given a free drink. The gaming tables also display signs with the minimum betting amount. Many Downtown casinos have lower minimum betting amounts than the larger casinos on the Strip. Maximum bets are also usually set by the casino.

Here are some of the ground rules for the most important games. For more details and variations, you should take a casino course or do some Internet research on sites such as *www.gamblingsites.org*. But to win the jackpot, you do not necessarily need a strategy or a game plan, just a healthy dose of luck!

GAMBLING

BLACKJACK

A variation of the card game known as 21. Each participant plays (for themselves) against the bank, represented by the dealer. Every player gets two cards, in some casinos face up, in others covered. The game leader always gets one face up and one covered card. Pictures count 10 points, aces 1 or 11 (as the player prefers), the other cards have the same value as their printed points. The aim is to get exactly 21 points – no more. Whoever gets 21 points with just two cards has a *blackjack* and wins one and a half of all the bets. Whoever has more points than the dealer but is still less than 21 points wins the size of the bet while those who are over 21 are bust and lose their bets. Choose a table and place your bet on the table, and start playing. Tap your finger on your card if you want more cards (*hit* or *draw*). Brush over your cards with a flat hand if you do not want anymore cards (*stand*). In many shops you can buy small *master strategy charts* that will give you a lot of tips.

CRAPS

At the craps table, emotions often run high. This is a fast-paced, loud dice game for extroverts and there is often a lot of screaming and shouting going on. A *shooter* has to throw two of the dice down hard (usually against a wall) for a certain number of points. You can either back the shooter and bet with him by placing your chips on the *pass line* or you can bet against him getting the right number of points and place your chips on the *don't pass bar* – obviously before the dice are thrown.

Now your intuition should tell you what the dice are going to do. If a seven or eleven is thrown, the shooter wins, as well as everyone who placed their chips on the pass line. If the result is two, three or twelve, the shooter loses, which means that those who placed their chips on the don't pass bar wins.

Every other point total gives the shooter the chance to throw exactly the same amount as soon as possible, or at least before he throws a seven. If he throws a

seven before a repeat of the previous point, the shooter (and everyone who bet with him) loses.

KENO

A lottery game with 80 numbers, players use a cross to mark off between one and fifteen numbers on the Keno forms. Enter how many marks you have made. Twenty numbers per round are drawn. After about ten minutes the results appear on the screens in casinos, coffee shops and restaurants. So it means that you can hit the Keno jackpot while enjoying a leisurely lunch. The size of the bet is entered as the price of the ticket. The aim is to get 15 correct numbers, all of which means that you need only luck and not any mathematical prowess. But depending on how many correct numbers you marked, you can win a multiple of the bet.

POKER

The game of the Wild West, the one that is played in every Western movie. It is played in so many variations, that only the ground rules will be explained here. Every player gets five cards. By exchanging cards you can get a certain combination or hand, for example a pair of triples (two or three cards that are worth the same), *full house* (a pair and a triple), a *straight* (five cards in sequence), *flush* (five cards of the same colour), *poker* (four cards of the same value) and the highest combination a *royal flush* (five cards in sequence and in the same colour). High stakes poker players are usually given separate VIP rooms so that they are not distracted and can concentrate in a more exclusive ambience.

ROULETTE

A small ball is thrown on a wheel with 38 numbered pockets. The players place their chips (often every participant has their own colour) on the table next to the wheel. While the French roulette is played with 37 numbered pockets, the American version has an extra 00, therefore 38 pockets. There are a variety of betting options for roulette players, you can place your chips on a single number or on the line between numbers and thus choose a combination of numbers. You can also bet on red or black, equal or unequal, the first 18 numbers or the last 18 numbers, the first 12, the middle 12 or the last 12 numbers. The dealer will call out *(rien ne va plus)* when no more bets will be accepted. Winnings can be up to 35 times the amount of the bet. The more possibilities you try to cover with a chip, the smaller the winnings.

SLOTS

This one is far too easy: simply put your money in and pull the lever (the lever arm is why it is also called a one-arm bandit). Nowadays they also come with a button instead of a lever, just press the button and the reels start spinning and hopefully your symbols all match up. Many one-arm bandits now have video screens (some with touch screens) and the old-fashioned mechanical varieties are hard to find.

It is a game of chance with the aim being to get all the same symbols or numbers in one row, when the machine stops. The paylines differs from machine to machine. Your odds of winning depend on how the machine has been set up by the operators. And they have planned very carefully where the lucky machines are placed. INSIDER TIP Ask the operators where luck strikes more often.

Many casinos now no longer have machines that make the classic pay out sound of coins (quarters) clattering into the tray, modern slot machines are operated with cards and not cash.

SPORT BETTING & HORSE RACING

Casinos show horse races and other sporting events on giant television screens live from all over the country, and of course they also take bets.

GOLF

If you play golf or would like to learn, Las Vegas is the perfect place. There are over 55 golf courses in the immediate vicinity.

At most of the courses you can hire clubs at very reasonable rates. During the heat of the summer you do not have to make a reservation but at other times it is better to book in advance (via the Internet or telephone).

Prices vary from $30 to $500 depending on the place, time of the year and time of the day. If you would like to play nine holes, ask about the affordable late afternoon or twilight rates. Appropriate clothing is requested at all the clubs: shirts with collars and pants and certainly no jeans or casual shorts. Normal gym shoes are accepted but no spiked golf shoes allowed. For more information see *www.lasvegas golf.com* and *www.lasvegasgolfcourses. com*.

GOLF COURSES

ANGEL PARK GOLF CLUB
(116 B3) *(ᗞ 0)*
A beautifully designed course with a magnificent view of the city and the mountains. *100 S. Rampart Blvd | tel. 702 2 54 46 53 | www.angelpark.com*

LAS VEGAS GOLF CLUB (116 B3) *(ᗞ 0)*
The oldest public golf course in Las Vegas, inexpensive but also very popular. *4300 W. Washington Ave | tel. 702 3 12 19 00 | www.lasvegasgc.com*

Manicured greens in the centre of the city – the Wynn Las Vegas golf course

TPC AT THE CANYONS (116 B3) *(ﾉﾉ O)*
Excellent venue for experienced golfers.
9851 Canyon Run Dr | tel. 702 2 56 25 00 |
www.tpc.com

WYNN LAS VEGAS
(112 C2) *(ﾉﾉ C–D7)*
The only venue INSIDER TIP inside a casino.
3131 S. Las Vegas Blvd | tel. 702 7 70 70 00 |
www.wynnlasvegas.com

GETTING MARRIED

● **Every year more than 90,000 weddings take place in Las Vegas, making it the wedding capital of the world. There is nowhere else where you can get married as quickly and as easily as here.**
A valid passport is almost all that you need. The bride and groom must appear in person in front of a clerk at the *Clark County Marriage Licence Bureau (201 E. Clark Ave)* in order to have a marriage license issued (at a cost of $60). The Bureau has very unusual office hours: *daily 8am–midnight*. There is also the option to complete the application form for a marriage licence 60 days in advance on the Internet: *www.clarkcountynv.gov/Depts/clerk*.
Divorced and widowed applicants must also submit the month, day, year and city of their divorce or death of their spouse, divorce papers help but they are not mandatory. Non USA citizens should also check with their own officials to ensure that the marriage certificate issued will also be recognised in their own country.
Same-sex marriages are not legal in Nevada, but a ceremony can still take place at any of the wedding chapels. Detailed information about the official

marriage conditions can be found on the Licence Bureau's websites *www.clark countynv.gov* and *www.visitlasvegas.com* (tel. 702 6 71 06 00).

Once the licence has been issued, the wedding ceremony can then be performed. This can be done simply and without any fuss or fanfare at the *Office of Civil Marriages* just a block away for a fee of $50 *(Sun–Thu 2pm–6pm, Fri/Sat 8am–10pm | 309 S. Third St)*. You do however, need to call beforehand: *tel. 702 6 71 05 77*. Or you can choose to get married in one of the dozens of Vegas wedding chapels. The wedding does require a witness but if you cannot bring anyone along, the chapel will provide one for you.

The majority of the wedding chapels have half-hour bookings but some also provide hour-long bookings. There is usually also an additional cost of about $50 for the minister's fee, which is separate from the fee charged by the chapel.

Whichever way you want to tie the knot, in Las Vegas anything and everything is possible: all in white, in tuxedos, in jeans or in a bikini, with a budget under $100 or more than $100,000, spontaneous or planned down to the last detail, with limousines and champagne or in a chip shop – each to their own, in the way that they want. There is an entire industry geared to weddings in Las Vegas so for information about the planning of the festivities – from limousine rentals, venues and DJs to photographers, caterers, jewellers and florists – you should consult the Internet under *www.vegas.com/weddings* or *www.showtimevegas.com/weddings. htm*.

Say 'yes' in half an hour – stretch limos queuing up in front of a wedding chapel

There you will also find the names of some wedding consultants, who will take care of all the planning. There are specialist companies for any and every sort of wedding: you can get married in a helicopter, with Elvis in attendance, at a drive-through chapel on a Harley Davidson, with no frills or completely over the top. On any day and at any time!

Should you decide to get married in Las Vegas, you will be in very good company. Many celebrities have sworn eternal love and said, 'Yes, I do' in Vegas, including Elvis and Priscilla Presley, Frank Sinatra and Mia Farrow, Bruce Willis and Demi Moore, Cindy Crawford and Richard Gere, Andre Agassi and Steffi Graf, as well as Brigitte Bardot, Paul Newman, Jon Bon Jovi and Mickey Rooney (on a number of occasions). And some of them are actually still to-gether. So do not let the big names intimidate you, but rather inspire you, just like the Licence Bureau sign that says, 'All wedding couples are celebrities to us!'

WEDDING CHAPELS

Apart from the specialised wedding chapels, all the themed hotels have their own wedding chapels and offer all the services that go with getting married. So you can get married on a Venetian gondola or at the Eiffel Tower.

GRACELAND CHAPEL (0) (*E2*)
Elvis and his music rule in the Graceland Chapel. Here couples are married by an Elvis impersonator who also escorts the bride and sings. *619 Las Vegas Blvd S. | tel. 702 3 82 00 91 | www.elvisweddings.com*

LITTLE CHURCH OF THE WEST (114 B3) (*B12*)
One of the oldest and most romantic chapels in the city with walls made of Californian redwood and atmospheric gas lanterns. *4617 S. Las Vegas Blvd | tel. 702 7 39 79 71 | www.littlechurchlv.com*

LITTLE WHITE CHAPEL (111 D4) (*E3*)
You do not even have to leave your car to say your, 'Yes, I do!' The world famous wedding chapel has a drive-up wedding window and a tunnel of love for weddings in a car, on a motorbike or in a white stretch limousine. *1301 S. Las Vegas Blvd | tel. 702 3 82 59 43 | www.alittlewhitechapel.com*

VIVA LAS VEGAS WEDDING CHAPEL (111 D3) (*E3*)
At this chapel your loved ones at home can watch the whole wedding ceremony via a live video feed over the Internet. Also weddings in the desert and other arrangements. *1205 Las Vegas Blvd S. | tel. 702 3 84 07 71 | www.vivalasvegasweddings.com*

TRAVEL WITH KIDS

Although Las Vegas makes its money with gambling, alcohol and sex – all things that parents try to keep away from their children – it also tries to maintain a balance between attracting families whilst keeping up its hedonistic image. Many venues do not allow children under 18, and children are banned by law from entering the casinos or anywhere where alcohol is served.

Despite this, children and adolescents will definitely not be bored in Vegas. Establishments like the *Excalibur* and *Circus Circus* offer entertainment for both adults and children alike. These hotels are very family-friendly so the hustle and bustle might not be as exciting for some adults. Some attractions for children are: the white tiger, dolphins and the volcano in the *Mirage*, the sharks in the *Mandalay Bay*, the lions in the *MGM Grand,* the *Ethel M. Chocolate Factory*, and the rides and 3D-adventures in the *Luxor*, *New York New York*, *Caesars Palace* and the *Stratosphere*. Certain rides have a minimum height or age requirement.

BABYSITTING

Nannies & Housekeepers USA offers qualified child care services. However, you will have to pay a rather hefty $45 per hour *(minimum 4 hours | tel. 702 4510021 | www.nahusa.com)*.

Grandma Dotti's Babysitting on the other hand is a rather more informal on-call service that charges $15 per hour for a babysitter to come to your hotel room *(minimum 3 hours | tel. 702 4561175)*. Generally hotels do not have babysitting services but will give you the number of an agency upon request.

CIRCUS CIRCUS (112 C1) (*Ø C6*)

Ever since it opened 1968 this hotel has housed a permanent circus where clowns, jugglers, trapeze artists and other top international artists perform every day in the small arena *(11am–midnight | free entrance | best to arrive 10 minutes before the show starts)*.

Behind the hotel is the *Adventuredome*, a giant glass amusement park with more than 20 different attractions including water slides, boat rides, climbing walls and mini golf *(times vary according to*

Sin City for the little ones: the fantasy-based, themed attractions of this adult playground are also ideal for children

season, as a guideline: Mon–Thu 10am–6pm, Fri/Sat 10am–midnight, Sun 10am–8pm | entrance free, day tickets for all the attractions $26.95). 2880 S. Las Vegas Blvd | tel. 702 7 94 39 39 | www.adventure-dome.com

EXCALIBUR (114 A1) (𝄞 B10)

Tournament of the Kings is a dinner show where you eat with your hands (as they did in the Middle Ages) and watch the kings of Europe fight the evil sorcerer Mordred at King Arthur's court. Blunt swords, but real horses and real pyrotechnics. *(Mon and Wed 6pm, Thu–Sun 6pm and 8.30pm | entrance from $57, food and soft drinks included | tel. 702 5 97 76 00). Also in Excalibur: the SpongeBob Square-Pants 4D Ride (Mon–Thu 11am–9pm, Fri 11am–10pm, Sat/Sun 10am–10pm | entrance $9.95). 3850 S. Las Vegas Blvd | www.excalibur.com*

LAS VEGAS NATURAL HISTORY MUSEUM (116 C3) (𝄞 O)

Coral reefs, thunder in the rain forest and dinosaur skeletons: lots to explore for young adventurers. In the *Young Scientist Center* children can even dig for dinosaur bones or search for Egyptian mummies. *Daily 9am–4pm | entrance $10, children $5 | 900 Las Vegas Blvd N. | tel. 702 3 84 34 66 | www.lvnhm.org*

INSIDER TIP LIED DISCOVERY CHILDREN'S MUSEUM ☺ (116 C3) (𝄞 O)

One of the best interactive museums for children where they can explore more than 100 exhibitions, including one about the desert and another called *Green Village* where they can learn about sustainability. *Tue–Fri 10am–4pm, Sat 10am–5pm, Sun noon–4pm | entrance $9.50, children $8.50 | 833 Las Vegas Blvd N. | tel. 702 3 82 54 37 | www.ldcm.org*

FESTIVALS & EVENTS

OFFICIAL HOLIDAYS

1 Jan *New Year's Day;* **4 July** *Independence Day;* **4th Thursday in Nov** *Thanksgiving;* **25 Dec** *Christmas.* The following are bank/public holidays when government offices, post offices and schools are closed, shops and museums on the other hand are open: **3rd Monday in Jan** *Martin Luther King Day;* **3rd Monday in Feb** *President's Day;* **last Monday in May** *Memorial Day;* **1st Monday in Sept** *Labor Day;* **2nd Monday in Oct** *Columbus Day;* **last Friday in Oct** *Nevada Day;* **11 Nov** *Veteran's Day*

FESTIVALS

FEBRUARY

▶ ***Chinese New Year:*** lions and dragons, dancing, acrobatics and Asian food. *Chinatown Plaza | 4255 Spring Mountain Rd | www.lvchinatown.com*
▶ ***Mardi Gras:*** street festival in Fremont Street and a party in the Orleans Casino

MARCH

▶ ***St Patrick's Day:*** on the 17th of March there are parades and block parties for the patron saint of Ireland. With some green clothing – at least a green hat – you will immediately be part of the fun. *Downtown | www.vegasexperience.com*

APRIL

▶ ***City of Lights Festival:*** big jazz festival with a view of the neon lights of the Strip. *Hills Park | Summerlin, in the northwest Las Vegas | www.yourjazz.com*
▶ ***Nevada Restaurant Association:*** hosted by the *Las Vegas International Hotel and Restaurant Show* – a culinary event with fine wines and delicacies prepared by the best chefs in the city. *www.nvrestaurants.com*
▶ ***Helldorado Days:*** end of April to mid-March Las Vegas celebrates its Wild West history with rodeos, parades and gunfire. *www.elkshelldorado.com*

SPRING & AUTUMN

▶ ***NHRA Nationals:*** for car fans – drag racing, hotrods and stock cars on the Las Vegas Speedway. *www.lvms.com*

MAY/JUNE

▶ ***Jazz in the Park:*** free jazz concerts in the *Clark County Amphitheatre. 500 S.*

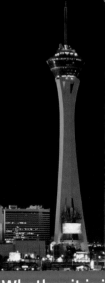

Whether it is jazz or folk music, rodeo, golf, carnival or Halloween – you will never be bored in Vegas

Grand Central Parkway | www.accessclark-county.com/parks

JUNE

▶ INSIDER TIP *Reggae in the Desert:* Caribbean music, drinks and food. *www.reggaeinthedesert.com*

▶ *World Series of Poker:* Las Vegas is the natural choice for the World Poker Championship: June to mid-July in the Rio Casino. *www.wsop.com*

▶ ⭐ *Miss USA:* the pageant takes place in the Planet Hollywood Casino and Las Vegas becomes the meeting place for the world's prettiest girls. *www.missuniverse.com*

JULY

▶ *Red White & Boom:* on the 4th of July, concerts, picnics, games and fireworks in the Desert Breeze Park. *8425 Spring Mountain Rd | www.redwhitenboom.com*

SEPTEMBER

▶ *Barrett Jackson Car Auction:* the annual vintage car auction takes place at the Mandalay Bay. *www.barrett-jackson.com*

OCTOBER

▶ INSIDER TIP *Halloween:* haunted houses and ghost parties – the best party is at the Hard Rock Hotel. *www.hardrockhotel.com*

▶ *Las Vegas Invitational:* annual golfing championship. *www.pgatour.com*

▶ *Shakespeare in the Park:* open-air Shakespeare plays. *Henderson Pavillon | Green Valley | www.hendersonlive.com*

DECEMBER

▶ INSIDER TIP *National Finals Rodeo:* for ten days Las Vegas becomes a cowboy city. *Thomas & Mack Center | 4505 Maryland Parkway | www.nfrexperience.com*

▶ *New Years Eve:* New Years Eve with kettledrums, trumpets and fireworks

LINKS, BLOGS, APPS & MORE

LINKS

▶ www.lasvegassun.com The website of the popular local newspaper the 'Las Vegas Sun' with insider information, tips about the latest events, new headline acts, the nightlife and interesting local news

▶ www.vegas4visitors.com An excellent resource with unbiased reviews about hotels, clubs, restaurants and events. There are also booking links and some useful information about planning your trip

▶ www.vegascoupons.com Great site with some amazing deals, discounts and even freebies

BLOGS & FORUMS

▶ www.lasvegasweekly.com The online version of the city guide with an events calendar, nightlife tips and links to some entertainment industry blogs. There is also a tab with a variety of guides, including one listing all the best DJs and pool parties

▶ www.lvrj.com The website for Nevada's largest daily newspaper, with local news, blogs and videos about Las Vegas. The section 'Best of Las Vegas' has listings for shows, restaurants and who is who in the city

▶ www.yelp.com/lasvegas This urban city guide is based on local opinions and reviews of all the best places to eat, to relax and the shows to see

APPS

▶ Vegas Way The best free app for the city, it tells you where to find everything you need: shows, casinos, restaurants, Wi-Fi hot spots or the nearest pharmacy. It comes bundled together with 20 smaller apps with loads of other listings

Regardless of whether you are still preparing your trip or already in Las Vegas: these addresses will provide you with more information, videos and networks to make your holiday even more enjoyable

APPS

▶ Cirque du Soleil **An app with all the show information you need, including seating plans, locations, special ticket promotions and more**

▶ Vegas Reality **This is a free augmented reality app from MGM Casinos with a lot of information about Las Vegas and its casinos**

▶ Vegas App **Another free app that even has the floor plans of casinos – so you won't get lost in the labyrinths of the massive themed hotels**

▶ Live Nation **An app that allows you to search for shows and clubs, you simply put Las Vegas in as your location and you will get all the entertainment listings as well as pre-sale specials and last minute tickets**

VIDEOS

▶ www.5min.com **Comprehensive online video library with a large selection of lifestyle videos about Las Vegas – simply type in Las Vegas and hit the 'find' button**

▶ casino-comps.info/2010/louis-theroux-gambling-in-las-vegas **To view the BBC documentary series about gambling in Las Vegas by the popular journalist Louis Theroux. It is a six-part series**

▶ www.ktnv.com **TV station with local news, Vegas video clips, weather, traffic and entertainment**

NETWORK

▶ www.couchsurfing.org **Get surfing and click your way into a private home in Las Vegas – connect with locals and experience the city in a more personal way. Not only is the bed (or couch) free but you also get to meet new people**

▶ forum.virtualtourist.com **An online travel community site where users share travel advice and their own experiences. Browse by location and interact with other tourists who have been to Las Vegas and who have some tips of their own to share**

TRAVEL TIPS

ARRIVAL

There are a number of charter companies that provide non-stop charter flights from major international cities directly to Las Vegas. Most national carriers also have regular scheduled flights from major international cities that are either direct or have a single transfer into Las Vegas. British Airways *(www.british airways.com)* and Virgin Atlantic *(www.virgin-atlantic.com)* fly non-stop from London to Las Vegas daily. Flights arrive at the *McCarran International Airport* (LAS) which is about a mile south of the edge of the Strip.

A taxi trip from the airport to the Strip will cost $12–20, to Downtown between $18–28. There are also various shuttle buses that cost about $6–7 as well as the city bus WAX from the airport to the Strip (corner Tropicana Ave) and to Downtown. Info: *www.mccarran.com*

RESPONSIBLE TRAVEL

It doesn't take a lot to be environmentally friendly whilst travelling. Don't just think about your carbon footprint whilst flying to and from your holiday destination but also about how you can protect nature and culture abroad. As a tourist it is especially important to respect nature, look out for local products, cycle instead of driving, save water and much more. If you would like to find out more about eco-tourism please visit: *www.ecotourism.org*

CAR HIRE

If you book from outside the United States, damage insurance (CDW) and additional third party cover are normally included, this can be expensive if booked after arrival. Some car hire firms have a minimum age requirement of 25 years. An international drivers' licence is sufficient.

Parking is not a problem: almost all the hotels offer free parking facilities. They also have the very practical free valet service. You drive up, hand the keys to the friendly young men and take a ticket. When leaving you give the valet a tip of $2–3 or $5 if he helps with your luggage.

CONSULATES & EMBASSIES

BRITISH-CONSULATE GENERAL LOS ANGELES
11766 Wiltshire Boulevard | Suite 1200 | Los Angeles | tel. +1 310 4 81 99 31 | ukin usa.fco.gov.uk/la

CANADIAN CONSULATE GENERAL LOS ANGELES
550 S. Hope St | 9th floor | Los Angeles | CA 90071 | tel. +1 213 3 46 27 00 | losangeles. gc.ca

CUSTOMS

The following goods can be imported duty-free into the USA: 200 cigarettes, 1 litre of alcohol over 22 per cent and gifts up to the value of $100. Many foodstuffs (fresh food, plants and seeds) may not be imported.

When returning to the EU, you may import 200 cigarettes or 50 cigars, 1 litre of alcohol over 22 per cent, 50ml perfume and other articles not totalling more than 390 pounds/430 euros.

ELECTRICITY

Mains voltage 110 Volt/60 Hertz. Small devices brought from Europe, like hair dryers or shavers, work with an adapter. Larger devices might require a transformer (available from electronics stores like Radio Shack) otherwise charging can take a long time.

EMERGENCY SERVICES

911 is the free emergency number. The operator directs you to the police, fire brigade or emergency doctor.

HEALTH

Ensure that you have International Health Insurance as treatment is very expensive in the USA. Accident and emergency departments (called emergency rooms, ER) are obliged to treat all patients but you have to pay up front with a credit card. Prescription medicines are obtained from a pharmacy while normal painkillers can be purchased at a drugstore. In emergencies, the hotel concierge will give you the name of the nearest day-clinic or call the paramedics.

IMMIGRATION

To travel to the United States without a visa you need to comply with the requirements of the Electronic System for Travel Authorization *(https://esta.cbp.dhs.gov)* by making an application at least 72 hours before starting your journey. Passports

CURRENCY CONVERTER

$	£	£	$
1	0.60	1	1.60
3	1.80	3	4.80
5	3	5	8
13	7.80	13	20.80
40	24	40	64
75	45	75	120
120	72	120	192
250	150	250	400
500	300	500	800

For current exchange rates see www.xe.com

issued after October 2005 must have a digital photo. Passports issued after October 2006 must be electronic passports with a digital chip containing biometric information. The ESTA approval is valid for two years. Children must have their own passport, and for a stay longer than three months a visa is required.

INFORMATION

LAS VEGAS CONVENTION & VISITORS AUTHORITY
United Kingdom Representative: *c/o Hills-Balfour | Colechurch House, 1 London Bridge Walk | SE1 2SX London | tel. +44 20 73 67 09 79*

LAS VEGAS VISITOR CENTERS
Locally the information office opposite the Convention Center will be able to assist you *(3150 Paradise Rd | tel. +1 702 8 92 75 75)* and the *Chamber of Commerce (6671 S. Las Vegas Blvd | suite 300 | tel.*

BUDGETING

Cola	60–80p/$1½–2½ for a glass
Steak	from £9/$15 as a main dish
Buffet	from £6/$10 for breakfast
Blackjack	£1.2–5½/$2–9 for a game
Taxi	from £8/$13 from the Strip to Downtown
Helicopter	from £40/$65 for a night flight over the Strip

+1702 7 35 16 16 | www.lvchamber.com). For guests arriving by car, there are info offices along the I 15 in Primm and Mesquite as well as on the US 93 in Boulder City.

INTERNET & WI-FI

All the hotels have Internet access but most of them do charge for access. Many coffee shops like Starbucks offer free online access – simply enquire at the counter. For a list of free Wi-Fi hot spots along the Strip www.lasvegas-how-to.com/las-vegas-free-wifi.php

MONEY & CREDIT CARDS

The American bills (which all look very similar) come in the following denominations: 1, 5, 10, 20, 50, 100 dollars. Coins in denominations of 1, 5, 10, 25, 50 cents and one dollar. Coins may also be referred to as follows: penny (1 cent), nickel (5 cents), dime (10 cents) and quarter (25 cents). The proverbial 'buck' equals one dollar. Visa and MasterCard are accepted almost everywhere, even for small amounts but

American Express is not as common. Make enquiries with your bank to check whether your debit card is valid for the US and whether you can use it to draw money at ATMs. Beware: ATMs in hotels and shops often charge a higher fee. You will need cash in small denominations for tips, bus or taxi fare. Taxi drivers are not obligated to give you change for notes higher than $20.

PHONE & MOBILE

Local calls from telephone booths cost 25–50 cents. The numbers 1800, 1866, 1877 and 1888 are mostly toll free within the USA. Hotels charge $1–2 when dialling these numbers. A cheaper alternative is to buy a prepaid phone card from a vending machine or shops like Walgreens or 7-Eleven.
Code for calling overseas from the US: 011 followed by country code, e.g. UK 0 11 44, Ireland 01 13 53. Code for calling the US and Canada: 001. Dial (*) for info and 0 for the operator.
Foreign mobile phones work in the United States only if they are GSM triband phones (remember to reset the phone to GSM). If you have one of these find out about roaming charges before you go. The snag is that you can incur very high roaming costs so it is worth getting a prepaid sim card for a local GSM network operator in the United States (Cellular One, T-Mobile USA, Verizon). You can also incur high charges from your mobile phone's messaging service. Best to switch if off even before you leave your home country!

PUBLIC TRANSPORT

BUS
The double decker, The Deuce (24 hours) and the chic, air-conditioned RTC buses of the Strip & Downtown Express (9am–

0.30am) take you up and down the Strip and Downtown. A trip costs $5 (careful, no change!), the day ticket $7 for the whole *RTC* network, a three day pass $20. More information: *www.rtcsnv.com*

MONORAIL

⏱ The environmentally friendly railway connects casinos on the eastern side of the Strip and takes you to the Convention Center (*trip $5, day ticket $12 | www.lv monorail.com*). There are also two free monorails that operate between Mandalay Bay–Luxor–Excalibur and Mirage–TI.

TAX

Prices are always shown without tax. Tax is only added when paying, for hotel rooms in Las Vegas 12 per cent and for goods 8.1 per cent.

TIME ZONE

Las Vegas falls under the Pacific Standard Time, the same time as California. So here it is eight hours earlier than in the UK. Summer time is from the second Sunday in March until the first Sunday in November. NB: these dates do not coincide with when the UK changes its clocks.

TIPPING

Visitors should remember that in the US tips are regarded as a part of the salary, not an added extra. The standard is 15–20 per cent of the amount (excluding tax). Bartenders and waitresses receive $1–2 per drink, porters $1–2 per piece of luggage, chamber maids $1–2 per day. If you should win something when gambling, it is a nice gesture to tip the dealer.

WEATHER IN LAS VEGAS

	Jan	Feb	March	April	May	June	July	Aug	Sept	Oct	Nov	Dec
Daytime temperatures in °C/°F	18/64	21/70	24/75	29/84	34/93	39/102	41/106	39/102	37/99	31/88	24/75	20/68
Nighttime temperatures in °C/°F	1/34	4/39	7/45	10/50	14/57	19/66	24/75	23/73	20/68	12/54	5/41	3/37
Sunshine hours/day	7	9	10	12	12	14	11	12	11	10	9	7
Precipitation days/month	3	3	2	1	0	1	3	3	2	2	2	3

NOTES

STREET ATLAS

Photo: Valley of Fire State Park

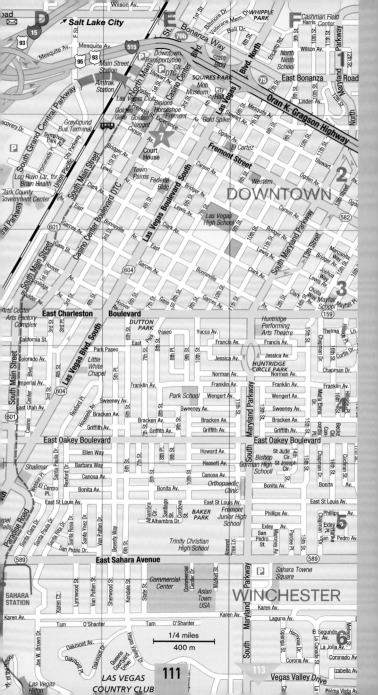

Dr.

New York-
New Y
A 112 **3**

MGM Grand
Lion Habitat
B MGM GRAND STATION

C

West Tropicana Avenue (593) East Tro

EXCALIBUR
STATION (604)
Tropicana America's
Best Value Inn
Motel 6

1 Excalibur
Mob Experience
Island Way
San
Remo
Koval Ln.
Duke Ellington Way
Dickow L

West Reno Av.
Desert Rose
Resort
East Reno Av.
East
Ali Baba
Ln.
Haven St.
Giles St.

2 Luxor
LUXOR
STATION

West Hacienda Av.
East
Hacienda
Av.
East Mandalay Bay Rd.
Danville Ln.
Bethel Ln.
Haven St.

Mandalay
Bay
Resort
MANDALAY BAY
STATION
Giles St.
Mesa
Vista Av.

Thehotel

Four
Seasons
Four Seasons Dr.
Haven Rd.

15

Dewey Dr.

3 West Russell Road

Clubhouse
Little Church
of the West

McCarran International Airp

Klondike
Haven St.

East Oquendo Rd.

Hughes Executive
Terminal Bldg.

Welcome to
Las Vegas
Sign

BALI HAI

4 GOLF COURSE

UP RR Henderson Branch Sierra Stone Lane

Post Rd.

Teco Av.
Windy Rd.
Ensworth St.

5 West Sunset Rd.
East Sunset Road (562)

All American
Sport Centre
Park
&
Ride
Gillespie St.
Pilot Rd.

CALLAWAY
Amelia
Earhart Ct.
Orville
Wright Ct.

Baker,
↓Los Angeles
Chamber of
Commerce (604)

GOLF CENTER
(PUBLIC)
SSTT
East Martin Av.

Town Square
Mall
La Cienega St.
Placid St.
East Pamalyn
Ave.

15

6 Hidden Well Road

Southern Las Vegas Beltway (215)

George Crockett Road

114

East Arby
East Arby Av.
Gillespie
East

D | **E** | **F**

Thomas & Mack Dr. | Dorothy Av. | Ct.

Swenson St. | Brussels St. | Dorothy Av. | Spencer St.

P | P | P | Elizabeth | **113** | Av.

East Tropicana Avenue | (593) **East Tropicana Avenue**

(605) Sage Av. | Paradise School | Bock St. | Shirley St. | Wilbur St. | Camelot Center | Tamarus St. | **1**

East Bell | Palo Verde Cir. | Las Vegas Villa | Radkovich Av. | Young St. | Lulu Av. | | East Reno Av.

Gus Guiffre Dr. | Toni Av. | Boyer St. | Toni Av. | Turner St. | Pattee Tamareno | Caliente St. | Crest Av. | Spencer St.

Palo Verde Rd. | Durante St. | Laramore Dr. | Reeder Dr. | Century Garden | Cir. | Cir. | Garden Cir. | Valley Glen St. | Mapleton Ln.

Rent a Car Rd. | Janis Ln. | Dalton Dr. | De Met Dr. | Marie St. | Golden Dr. | | East Hacienda Av. | Escondido St. | Tamarus St. | **2**

Kitty Hawk Way | Monika Way | East Hacienda Av. | Wilbur St. | Manos Ct. | Ward School | Caliente Ct. | Papaya Ct. | Lindero Pl. | Sandalwood Dr.

Prince Salty St. | Westminster Av. | Count Wutzke Av. | King Richard Av. | Viscount Carlson Ct. | Princess Katy Av. | Caliente St. | Caliente Ct.

Wayne Newton Blvd. | Lady Marlene Av. | Rawhide St. | Di Blasi Dr. | Fraya Dr.

Customs | **East Russell Road**

P | Mayne Newton Blvd. | P | P | Kelly Ln. | P | P

Silver Garage | Gold Garage | Russell Rd. | East Landing Strip Av. | Spencer St. | **3**

ninal) | Wright Brothers Ln. | **PARADISE**

ate B | Gate C | Gate D | **4**

Airport Tunnel

ast Sunset Road | **East Sunset Road** | (562) | Spencer St. | **5**

Trade Center Dr. | Grier Dr. | Kelly Johnson Dr. | Paradise Road | Escondido | South Maryland Parkway

Pilot Rd. | Grier Dr. | (605) | East Heim Av. | 1/4 miles

Caballo Rd. | UP RR Henderson Branch Sierra Stone Lane | Pat St. | 400 m

Pamalyn Av. | Grand Canyon | East Pama Ln. | **6**

8 | Pilot Rd. | Finale Ln. | Spencer St.

outhern Las Vegas Beltway | **115** | Operetta Way | Duet Ct. | Rust Dr. | Garden Path Ct. | Bright View Dr.

White | Chaparral Rd. | Recital Way | White Dr. | Tamarus St. | Beech Grove Dr. | Birch Creek

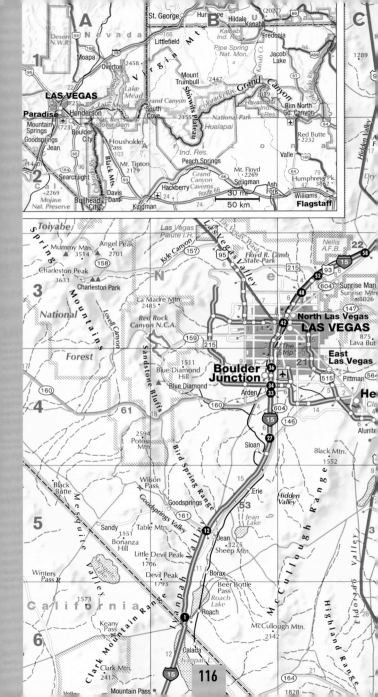

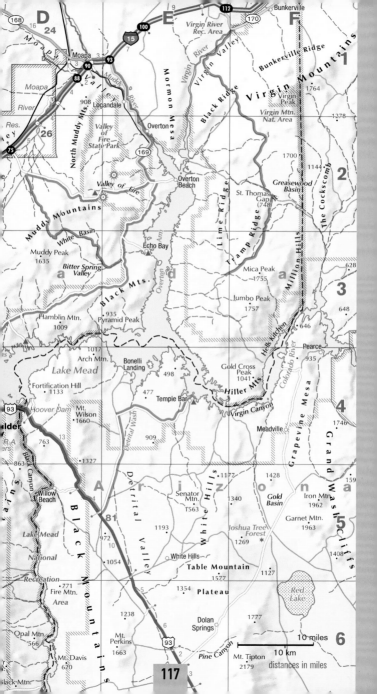

117

This index lists a selection of the streets and squares shown in the street atlas

KEY TO STREET ATLAS

★ Point of interest
Sehenswürdigkeit
Curiosité
Curiosità
Curiosidad

✈ Int'l. Airport
Int. Flughafen
Aéroport int.
Aeroporto int.
Aeropuerto int.

Monorail
Monorail
—•— Monorail
Monorail
Monorail

M̂ Museum
Museum
Musée
Museo
Museo

✈ Airfield
Flugplatz
Aérodrome
Aerodromo
Aeródromo

� Monument
Denkmal
Monument
Monumento
Monumento

👓 Theatre
Theater
Théâtre
Teatro
Teatro

🚌 Bus station
Busbahnhof
Station d'autobus
Stazione autolinee
Estación de autobuses

✝ Church
Kirche
Église
Chiesa
Iglesia

🎬 Cinema
Kino
Cinéma
Cinema
Cine

P Car park
Parkplatz
Parking
Parcheggio
Aparcamiento de
varios pisos

⛺ Camping site
Campingplatz
Terrain de camping
Campeggio
Camping

🗼 Tower
Turm
Tour
Torre
Torre

✉ Post office
Postamt
Poste
Posta
Oficina de correos

Notable building
Bemerkenswertes Geb.
Édifice remarquable
Edificio notevole
Edificio notable

ℹ Information
Information
Informations
Informazione
Información

⊕ Hospital
Krankenhaus
Hôpital
Ospedale
Hospital

Public buildings
Öffentliche Gebäude
Édifice public
Edificio pubblico
Edificio público

📖 Library
Bibliothek
Bibliothèque
Biblioteca
Biblioteca

✿ Police
Polizei
Police
Polizia
Policía

Department store
Kaufhaus
Grand magasin
Grande magazzino
Grandes almacenes

◁ One-way road
Einbahnstraße
Rue à sens unique
Strada a senso unico
Calle de sentido único

.⌒ Golf
Golf
Golf
Golf
Golf

Hotel
Hotel
Hôtel
Albergo
Hotel

MARCO POLO Highlights

INDEX

This index lists all sights, hotels, restaurants, malls, clubs und shows featured in this guide. Numbers in bold indicate a main entry.

WRITE TO US

e-mail: info@marcopologuides.co.uk

Did you have a great holiday?
Is there something on your mind?
Whatever it is, let us know!
Whether you want to praise, alert us
to errors or give us a personal tip –
MARCO POLO would be pleased to
hear from you.
We do everything we can to provide the
very latest information for your trip.

Nevertheless, despite all of our authors'
thorough research, errors can creep in.
MARCO POLO does not accept any
liability for this. Please contact us by
e-mail or post.

MARCO POLO Travel Publishing Ltd
Pinewood, Chineham Business Park
Crockford Lane, Chineham
Basingstoke, Hampshire RG24 8AL
United Kingdom

PICTURE CREDITS
Cover photograph: The Stratosphere Casino Tower (Huber: Giovanni Simeone)
W. Dieterich (front flap left, front flap right, 2 centre top, 3 top, 3 centre, 3 bottom, 6, 8, 30, 34, 36, 38, 39, 40, 42, 58, 61, 62/63, 64, 66, 68/69, 72, 77, 78/79, 85, 86, 88/89, 94/95, 96/97, 100 bottom, 101, 108/109); DuMont Bildarchiv: Frischmuth (7, 10/11, 90, 100 top), Leue (99); Earth Limos & Buses (16 bottom); N. Fraatz (23); Huber: Giovanni Simeone (1 top); ©iStockphoto.com: James Camp (16 top), Paul Erickson (16 centre); Jennifer Main Gallery (17 top); Laif/Arcaid: Tepper (33); Laif/Aurora: Judge (9, 74); Laif/hemis.fr: Frumm (97); Laif/Redux/The New York Time: Brekken (98); Laif: Falke (76), Heeb (98/99), hemis.fr (96); Look: Fleisher (14/15); mauritius images/FreshFood: NtJDO (60 left); mauritius images/Oredia: Tombini (60 right); mauritius images: Alamy (20, 48, 52); K. Teuschl (1 bottom, 2 top, 2 centre bottom, 2 bottom, 4, 5, 13, 18/19, 24 left, 24 right, 25, 26/27, 45, 46, 50/51, 55, 57, 70, 80, 83, 93, 121); Viva Las Vegas: Robert Dix DBA Cherry Club Photography (17 bottom)

1st Edition 2013
Worldwide Distribution: Marco Polo Travel Publishing Ltd, Pinewood, Chineham Business Park, Crockford Lane, Basingstoke, Hampshire RG24 8AL, United Kingdom. Email: sales@marcopolouk.com
© MAIRDUMONT GmbH & Co. KG, Ostfildern
Chief editors: Michaela Lienemann (concept, managing editor), Marion Zorn (concept, text editor)
Author: Sabine Stamer; co-author: Karl Teuschl; editor: Marlis v. Hessert-Fraatz
Programme supervision: Ann-Katrin Kutzner, Nikolai Michaelis, Silwen Randebrock
Picture editors: Gabriele Forst, Barbara Schmid
What's hot: wunder media, Munich
Cartography street atlas: © MAIRDUMONT, Ostfildern; Cartography pull-out map: © MAIRDUMONT, Ostfildern
Design: milchhof : atelier, Berlin; Front cover, pull-out map cover, page 1: factor product munich
Translated from German by Wendy Barrow; editor of the English edition: Margaret Howie, fullproof.co.za
Prepress: M. Feuerstein, Wigel

DOS & DON'TS ✋

There are laws even in Sin City!

DON'T LEAVE THE CITY WITHOUT HAVING GAMBLED

You don't have to be a high roller, but visiting Las Vegas and its casinos and not having a try at gambling is only half the fun. And if everyone did that, Las Vegas would not exist.

DO WAIT FOR YOUR TABLE

Do wait at the restaurant entrance for the hostess to escort you to your table. Of course you may ask if you would prefer to sit somewhere else.

DON'T TRAVEL WITHOUT A JERSEY

It is hard to believe but you should always take a jersey or a jacket with you (especially in midsummer) as the large casinos – like for example, the Venetian – have very chilly temperatures and after two days you may come down with a cold.

DO TURN OFF YOUR MOBILE PHONE

Player etiquette – it is absolutely taboo to let your mobile phone ring at the playing tables, or worse still, to answer it.

DON'T FORGET YOUR PASSPORT

Drinking alcohol and gambling is only legal over 21. Children and adolescents under 18 are not allowed inside the casinos. All under-18s need to have adult supervision after 9pm on the Strip (away from the Strip after 10pm). Many bars require identification.

DO BE CAREFUL

On the Strip and in the Fremont Street Experience, you have nothing to fear. But do not go for walks alone at night down isolated streets. Always walk in pairs or groups, when leaving the busy areas, or take a taxi.

DON'T DISTURB THE PROS

Dealers are very helpful and will gladly help you with the rules and secrets of the game. But do not ask any questions at tables packed with stressed-out and sweaty high rollers.

DO TAKE WATER

It is essential to always have enough drinking water with you when you go on an excursion in the area. During summer it gets extremely hot and you can dehydrate quite quickly.

DON'T DRINK ALCOHOL ON THE STREETS

You are allowed to down a cold beer in the heat – just not on the street. You are not even allowed to walk around with a sealed case of beer or bottle of wine. Alcohol always has to be in a package.